Andrew Mckie, Barrister at Clerksroom Manchester, is a specialist in claimant and defendant personal injury, travel and housing law practitioner. Andrew practices in personal injury, disease, travel and housing law including housing disrepair and cavity wall claims.

Andrew practices from Clerksroom Manchester (0845 083 3000) or bookings@clerksroom.com or www.clerksroom.com.

Personal Injury 2019 – Updates, Cases and Key Decisions

Personal Injury 2019 – Updates, Cases and Key Decisions

Andrew Mckie,
Barrister at Law, Clerksroom (Manchester),
LLB Hons, PG DIP and
Former Solicitor Advocate,
Personal Injury, Fraud, Credit Hire

Law Brief Publishing

Published 2019 by Law Brief Publishing, an imprint of Law Brief Publishing Ltd
30 The Parks
Minehead
Somerset
TA24 8BT

www.lawbriefpublishing.com

Paperback: 978-1-912687-28-2

PREFACE

The aim of the book is to provide an updated summary of important 2018/2019 cases in the ever developing areas of personal injury. It is an area that is undergoing rapid change and with many new decisions the author hopes that the book assists the reader to navigate some of these issues in an easy to digest format. All law and cases are up-to-date as of 1st September 2019.

Andrew Mckie
Clerksroom
September 2019

CONTENTS

Chapter One	Costs, CFA and Retainers – Updates, Cases and Key Decisions	1
Chapter Two	Useful Fixed Costs Cases	15
Chapter Three	OL/PL – Updates, Cases and Key Decisions	33
Chapter Four	NIHL Claims – Updates, Cases and Key Decisions	71
Chapter Five	Disease Claims – Updates, Cases and Key Decisions	89
Chapter Six	EL Claims – Updates, Cases and Key Decisions	99
Chapter Seven	The PI Claims Market – An Overview of the Changes	107

CHAPTER ONE

COSTS, CFA AND RETAINERS – UPDATES, CASES AND KEY DECISIONS

CFAs and Success Fees

There are now a number of new services advising clients to go back and check if their legal fees were charged correctly. A new breed of claim is from clients challenging success fees (especially in PI and clinical negligence litigation) under the Solicitors Act 1974 (section 70). This is causing a headache for the PI sector.

Solicitors in the PI and Clinical Negligence sector must be aware of these issues and plan accordingly. Contrary to popular belief there is no automatic right to charge the client the standard 25% deduction from damages under LASPO, and the success fee charged can be subject to an assessment. There may be a problem where Solicitors have charged a success fee of 25%, particularly on low value road traffic accidents, where no risk assessment was undertaken at the outset of the case.

The benefit for the lawyers running these cases to challenge success fees, is that often the loser pays the costs of the assessment and it may be only £500 or so that is challenged and it may make it uneconomical to fight. The costs of any assessment will be paid by the client unless the solicitor's costs are reduced by more than one fifth in which case the solicitor will pay the client's costs of the assessment process. This rule is subject to two exceptions: (i) where the assessment is on application by the solicitor and the paying party does not attend or (ii) where the court orders otherwise either as part of the order for the assessment or where the circumstances in section 70(10) apply.

CFAs and Risk Assessments

Herbert v HH Law Ltd [2018] EWHC 580 (QB)

The client, who had been injured in a road traffic accident, had entered into a CFA with the firm which provided that, if successful, she was to pay its basic charges, disbursements, ATE premium and 100% success fee. The claim was submitted via the RTA portal and the client accepted a Pt 36 offer of £3,400 plus costs. From that sum, the firm deducted £1,178, comprising costs of £829 and an ATE premium of £349. The client then instructed her current solicitor (JG), which challenged the billed costs, contending, in particular, that the firm had not conducted a risk assessment justifying the 100% success fee.

A district judge had been right to reduce a solicitor's success fee from 100% to 15%. The fact that the client had entered into a CFA which set out the success fee percentage did not mean that they had approved that percentage within the meaning of CPR r.46.9(3).

The court said in that case:-

> *'15. I do not accept that any of those relevant factors are sufficient in addition to the circumstances of the case, the nature of the claim, and the evidence from the Claimant to justify an uplift of 100%.* ***It is difficult to see in the circumstances of this case known to the solicitors at the time that the CFA was to be entered into that an uplift of much more than 12.5% could ever be justified.*** *On the circumstances described by the client the facts of the case was straightforward, the nature of the injury was minor soft tissue damage and whiplash, there was no time off work, and it was likely this case would be settled for a modest amount in a short period of time.'* ***In the circumstances of the particular case, and allowing for the fact that the 'modest' disbursements were funded by the solicitors for a 'fairly short' period, the appropriate success fee was 15%, namely £276 plus VAT = £331.20.***

Challenges are emerging to the success fees

A and M v Royal Mail Group [2015] EW Misc B24 (CC)

The court refused an application for success fees and after the event insurance premiums to be paid out of damages obtained by children in a personal injuries settlement. The solicitors had failed to carry out a risk assessment of the prospects of winning and had failed to adequately advise the litigation friend about funding arrangements or why the funding model had been employed, or to give details of any agreed costs.

The Court said in that case:-

> *"In his final report Sir Rupert Jackson recommended that General Damages recovered in a case where a CFA was entered into after 1 April 2013 should be increased by 10% to compensate any Claimant for the additional irrecoverable expense of a success fee. Following the Court of Appeal decision in Simmons v Castle that enhancement has taken effect. The skeleton argument from Scott Rees in this case refers to the quote from the economic assessor to Sir Rupert Jackson's Inquiry, Professor Paul Penn, that the increase in general damages will in the great majority of cases leave Claimant's no worse off.* ***That clearly demonstrates that it was not within the contemplation of either Sir Rupert Jackson or Professor Penn that the success fee would always be equivalent to 25% of the damages or indeed that that would be the norm. On the contrary it would appear that it was contemplated that the success fee would seldom be equivalent to 25% of the damages****"*

Risk Assessments – some tips

Some practical tips:-

- Ensure each case has a risk assessment as to how the success fee was reached on each case. The risk assessment must be tailored to the facts.

- Ensure the risk assessment is signed off by a senior lawyer and can be justified.

- Even RTA cases should be subject to a risk assessment.

- Consider whether on for example a passenger RTA needs to charge a success fee of 25%. Some Courts will only allow 5% see A & B -v- The Royal Mail Group [2015]

- If your firm is faced with a claim see section 70 - the powers are limited:-

  "Where an application under subsection (2) is made by the party chargeable with the bill—

  (a) after the expiration of 12 months from the delivery of the bill, or

  (b) after a judgment has been obtained for the recovery of the costs covered by the bill, or (c) after the bill has been paid, but before the expiration of 12 months from the payment of the bill.

  no order shall be made except in special circumstances and, if an order is made, it may contain such terms as regards the costs of the assessment as the court may think fit." (emphasis added).

- If the success fee changes, make sure the client is updated.

- Make sure the basis and level of the success fee, is properly explained to the client at the outset of the case.
- Also consider ATE on low value RTA cases - especially minor cases- is the premium reasonable as compared to the risk? The client must be advised.

QWOCS AND COSTS including disapplication of qwocs, fundamental dishonesty, set off and exemptions

Pre-action disclosure applications are not protected by QOCS, nor are proceedings where a claimant has entered into a pre-commencement funding arrangement, which is defined in:-
48.2(1)

A pre-commencement funding arrangement is-

- *(i) a funding arrangement as defined by rule 43.2(1)(k)(i) where......"*
- *CPR 43.2(1)(k)(i) defines a funding arrangement as "an arrangement where a person has –*
- *(i) entered into a conditional fee agreement or a collective conditional fee agreement which provides for a success fee.....".*

Important point – if you issue a PAD consider if you therefore need ATE to cover the risk of adverse costs. The default position in a PAD application is that the applicant pay the costs. Very important on non-fixed costs cases.

QWOCS exemptions

> *Exceptions to qualified one-way costs shifting where permission not required*
>
> *44.15 Orders for costs made against the claimant may be enforced to the full extent of such orders without the permission of the court where the proceedings have been struck out on the grounds that –*
>
> *(a) the claimant has disclosed no reasonable grounds for bringing the proceedings;*
>
> *(b) the proceedings are an abuse of the court's process; or*
>
> *(c) the conduct of –*
>
> *(i) the claimant; or*
>
> *(ii) a person acting on the claimant's behalf and with the claimant's knowledge of such conduct, is likely to obstruct the just disposal of the proceedings.*

Let's look at some examples…

No Reasonable grounds for bringing proceedings

Some possible examples:-

- C issues the claim without a valid cause of action.
- C issues against the wrong Defendant.
- C issues pleading the wrong cause of action.

NB important before issue :-

- Check you have the correct Defendant.

- Check you have pleaded the correct cause of action – on complex cases refer to Counsel.
- Check you have a valid cause of action!

Abuse of process

Potential examples:-

- The proceedings are issued with an incorrect issue fee i.e. deliberately underpaying the claim.
- The claim has been issued a second time for the same cause of action after the first was struck out.
- The claim is struck out for procedural irregularity such as failing to serve in time.
- NB if the case is struck out, D will likely apply to disapply QWOCS.

Some tips:-

- Ensure extra attention of is paid to potential issues of strike out especially serving proceedings in time and issuing very near to limitation.
- No ATE will likely cover such as costs order and will end up being borne by the firm.

QWOCS – some practical tips

1. Ensure the claimant is provided with a QWOCS warning at the outset in writing.
2. Repeat the warning at keys stages such as issuing proceedings, letter before action / CNF stages and witness evidence.

3. Makes sure the client understands how QWOCS operates.

4. QWOCs is not a free pass to issue poor cases.

5. Procedural compliance is very important.

CPR 44.16

Exceptions to qualified one-way costs shifting where permission required:-

> *44.16*
>
> *(1) Orders for costs made against the claimant may be enforced to the full extent of such orders with the permission of the court where the claim is found on the balance of probabilities to be fundamentally dishonest.*

Claimant Lawyers have to be wary of the rules surrounding fundamental dishonesty. In the case of **Gosling v Screwfix and Anr** (unreported, 29 March 2014) at Cambridge County Court, HHJ Moloney QC ordered the claimant to pay the defendant's costs of the action on an indemnity basis.

The Judge ruled that a personal injury claimant who exaggerated the extent of his ongoing symptoms should be denied the protection of qualified one-way costs shifting (QOCS) on the grounds that the claim was "fundamentally dishonest".

In Bain v Zurich [2015] the Court said:-

> *"What it comes to is this: what does fundamentally dishonest mean? It does not, in my judgment, cover situations where there is simply exaggeration or embellishment. It is not unknown for these courts to hear claimants who appear to have suffered injury but who, whether*

consciously or otherwise, overstate the extent of their injuries. Therefore, for example, commonly, a soft tissue injury of the neck or back may be said to be more severe than a court concludes it actually was. That would not be fundamentally dishonest. Equally, in the experience of these courts, from time to time, schedules of loss are presented which somewhat magnify the degree of disability, for example, exaggerating the need for help with gardening and DIY and claiming an excessive number of hours Again, generally speaking, I would not regard a schedule of loss, which rather exaggerates the claim for loss of services, to amount to being fundamentally dishonest.

Having said that, these cases are fact sensitive and there may be situations where if a claim is patently and obviously exaggerated, the sole purpose being to recover damages to which a claimant is not entitled, it may be that a judge concludes that that renders the claim fundamentally dishonest"

Qwocs and dishonesty – some tips

1. Ensure the client is given an FD warning at the outset and at various point in the case.

2. FD for qwocs exemption does not have to be pleaded, so be alive to the risks.

3. If the client is at risk of a finding of FD, clear and proper advice must be given.

4. The Court will be critical of a claimant whom runs a case where FD is found – especially where D has given an early warning they would be seeking such a finding.

5. If C seeks to discontinue do this as early as possible and not just before Trial. A Judge is more likely to allow C to find FD where C discontinues late in the day with no reason (where FD has been alleged).

QWOCS and multiple defendants

In *Cartwright v Venduct Engineering Ltd [2018] EWCA Civ 1654*, the claimant issued proceedings against six named defendants for noise induced hearing loss (NIHL). The third defendant, Venduct, accepted that it was responsible for any liability that was established on the part of the first and second defendants.

The claimant then settled with the fourth, fifth and sixth defendants, who agreed to pay him £20,000. This was recorded in a Tomlin order. The claimant then served a notice of discontinuance in respect of the claim against Venduct.

Venduct sought its costs of £8,000 from the claimant; under the QOCS rule 44.14(1), a successful defendant can enforce a costs order up to the damages recovered by the claimant.

At first instance, Regional Costs Judge Hale in Nottingham held that the Tomlin order did not meet the requirement of the rule that such costs could only be paid from an *"order for damages and interest. The schedule to a Tomlin order was not an order of the court"*.

He also ruled that Venduct would have been entitled under rule 44.14, in principle, to enforce its costs order against the claimant, even though the source of the claimant's funds was another defendant. The Court said:-

> *"For the reasons explained below, I consider that each of these ways of testing the underlying dispute between the parties about multi-defendant cases leads to the conclusion that the Costs Judge was correct when he concluded that Venduct were, in principle, entitled to enforce its costs order against the claimant, even though the source of the claimant's funds was another defendant.*
>
> *Let us assume that the claimant issued proceedings against two defendants, A and B, which went all the way to trial. The claimant recovered £100,000 against defendant A, but the claim against*

defendant B failed, leading B to incur £40,000 by way of costs. In circumstances where the claimant had freely sued B (so that a Bullock or Sanderson order was inappropriate), I can see no reason in principle why B should not recover the £40,000 from the £100,000 payable by A to the claimant.

The QOWCS regime is designed to ensure that a claimant does not incur a net liability as a result of his or her personal injury claim: that, at worst, he or she has broken even at the end of the action. In the example I have given, the QOWCS regime will have facilitated his recovery of £100,000 against A. But there is no reason why that regime should prevent B from recovering its costs out of the damages payable by A.

Any other result would give a claimant carte blanche to commence proceedings against as many defendants as he or she likes, requiring those defendants to run up large bills by way of costs, whilst remaining safe in the knowledge that, if the claim fails against all but one defendant, he or she will incur no costs liability of any kind to the successful defendants, despite the recovery of sums by way of damages from the unsuccessful defendant. That seems to me to be wrong in principle, because it would encourage the bringing of hopeless claims.

The wording of the rule is consistent with that approach. There is nothing in r.44.14(1) which suggests that the claimant's fund (out of which the costs order will be met) is specific to the damages and interest payable by the defendant seeking to enforce the costs order, as opposed to the damages and interest payable by any other defendant. No such limitation can be discerned, and on the contrary, r.44.14(1) deals simply with orders for costs made against a claimant on the one hand, and orders for damages and interest made in favour of the claimant, on the other. The language is wide. It is clearly capable of embracing the situation in which defendant B has a claim for costs against the claimant which does not exceed the amount of the order for damages and interest made in favour of the claimant and payable by defendant A".

Key points:

1. Make sure that if you issue against multiple defendants there is a valid cause of action against each.

2. Speculative claims against more than one defendant may result in a costs order C has to pay from damages.

3. Before discontinuing seek no order as to costs or ask the Court to consider a Sanderson or Bullock order.

QWOCS and Discontinuing

WAYNE ROUSE v AVIVA INSURANCE LTD (2016)

The procedure to be adopted in conducting CPR r.44.16 applications where the case had been discontinued was a matter for the court's discretion. There could be circumstances in which it was proportionate for there to be a trial to determine the issue of fundamental dishonesty. Where a claimant did not give evidence, or did not proffer any reason for the decision to discontinue, then the defendant could invite the court to draw an adverse inference.

Shaw v Medtronic Corevalve LLC & Others [2017] EWHC 1397 (QB)

The Fifth Defendant sought an order setting aside the Notice of Discontinuance, so as to allow the court to consider striking out the claim on the basis that the Claimant had no reasonable grounds for bringing the proceedings.

That would have the effect of bringing the matter back within the CPR 44.15(1)(a) exception to QOCS.

The judge refused, saying that:

"... the Claimant had a right to discontinue under CPR rule 38.2. It was a proper use of that power, and to be encouraged, for the Claimant to recognise ... that her claim against the Fifth Defendant was not sustainable and to discontinue that claim (Paragraph 53)."

The court recognised that it had power under CPR 38.4 to set aside a Notice of Discontinuance and the authorities suggested that that should only be done if there had been an abuse of process in serving the Notice of Discontinuance. The rule itself is silent as to when the power should be exercised. The judge held that the facts here were not an abuse of process ***"or anything sufficient to justify setting aside the Notice of Discontinuance (Paragraph 58)."***

<u>QWOCS and set off</u>

On a multiple claimant case, can damages of one claimant be set off against another where another C fails?

CPR 44.12 says:-

Set Off

44.12

(1) Where a party entitled to costs is also liable to pay costs, the court may assess the costs which that party is liable to pay and either –

a. *set off the amount assessed against the amount the party is entitled to be paid and direct that party to pay any balance; or*

b. *delay the issue of a certificate for the costs to which the party is entitled until the party has paid the amount which that party is liable to pay*

In Darini and another v Markerstudy Group

HHJ Dight considered this question. He held that CPR 44 Section II was a self-contained code and was to be contrasted to Section I of CPR 44, which necessarily created a different procedural environment for the costs of personal injury claims.

He concluded that, under the QOCS regime, a defendant can only enforce a costs order (which includes setting off of that costs order) in the manner indicated in CPR 44.14, 44.15 and 44.16, and that these rules limited the court's discretion and the power to order set-off contained in CPR 44.12 in the context of QOCS. Because the circumstances in CPR 44.15 and CPR 44.16 were not in play, and the court was not seeking to set off costs against damages and interest, it had no power to order set-off.

CHAPTER TWO
USEFUL FIXED COSTS CASES

NICOLE CHAPMAN v TAMESIDE HOSPITAL NHS FOUNDATION TRUST (2016)

A defendant which had failed to comply with the Pre-Action Protocol for Personal Injury Claims was ordered to pay the claimant's costs. The defendant had asserted that it had no documents to disclose pre-issue, but subsequently disclosed relevant documents, causing the claimant to discontinue her claim and she was awarded her full costs on an OL claim. This is an important decision of post Jackson cases where early disclosure of documents are withheld and disclosed late in the day.

The Judgment said:-

1. *This has been the hearing of an unusual application, certainly not one which I have come across before. I said somewhat flippantly just before lunch that Deputy District Judge Herzog should have acceded to the parties' application, yesterday, to take this matter before a regional costs judge which would have avoided my having to address this novel but somewhat thorny issue. However I am entirely satisfied it was appropriate for me to deal with it and Judge Herzog's decision was entirely correct.*

2. ***It's an occupier's liability claim. The Claimant alleges that she went to the Defendant's A & E Department and whilst there she slipped on a leaflet on the floor (quite probably a solicitor's leaflet advertising their services), as a result of which she fell and incurred injuries which are set out in the report, which is on the file, from Dr Ballin.***

3. *Occupier's liability claims now, of course, are commenced in the Portal but this case it dropped out of the Portal. Therefore Part 7 proceedings were issued and they proceeded in a fairly normal*

fashion, but close to trial they were discontinued and that discontinuance followed some discussions between the parties' solicitors. As a result they sent a consent order to the Court on 8th April, which I had to amend because it provided at paragraph 2:

(It is ordered that) "the Claimant withdraws her claim for damages."

Of course, the Court has got no power to do that, a common error, but being somewhat pedantic I simply converted that into a recording that the Claimant withdrew her claim for damages, but the crucial part of the order was at paragraph 2 of the order as issued:

"The Claimant's entitlement to costs (if any) pursuant to CPR 44.2 and 44.11 and the level of those costs should be dealt with by a hearing, 15th June at 11 a.m."

4. ***The provisions of CPR 44.11 are not in fact germane, though they relate to misconduct in relation to assessment proceedings, but the relevant consideration is, of course, CPR 44.2. That starts off headed: "The Court's discretion as to costs, 44.21:***

> ***"(1) The Court has discretion as to –***
>
> > ***(a) whether costs are payable by one party to another;***
> >
> > ***(b) the amount of those costs; and***
> >
> > ***(c) when they are to be paid."***

And it goes on at 44.2.4:

> ***"In deciding what order (if any) to make about costs, the Court will have regard to all the circumstances, including –***
>
> > ***(a) the conduct of all the parties;"***

And 44.2.5:

"The conduct of the parties includes –

(a) conduct before, as well as during, the proceedings and in particular the extent to which the parties followed the Practice Direction – Pre- Action Conduct or any relevant pre-action protocol;

(b) whether it was reasonable for a party to raise, pursue or contest a particular allegation or issue;

(c) the manner in which a party has pursued or defended its case or a particular allegation or issue; and

(d) whether a Claimant who has succeeded in the claim, in whole or in part, exaggerated its claim."

But of course, that final provision is not germane to the issues here.

And what the Claimant says is that the Defendant's conduct in dealing with this claim has been such that the Court ought to implement the punitive provisions of 44.2.4 and

The provision of that part of the rules is designed to be part of the Court's cost controlling mechanism and to provide a means whereby the Court can impose a penalty on a party who has mis-conducted litigation. And it does have to be said really here, that the Defendant's conduct of this matter has been entirely unacceptable and egregious. It is typified by the first letter in the bundle.

6. *The situation here was that this was not an unusual claim. It was a claim by somebody who had gone into the Defendant's premises and slipped as a result, she would say, of contamination of the floor. So it is not an unusual or exotic claim, it's the kind of claim which the Courts are fully familiar with and which practitioners dealing with these matters should also be fully familiar with.*

7. *The matter is now being dealt with on behalf of the Defendant by Weightmans. At that stage it was being dealt with by the NHS Litigation Authority and I hazard a guess at the number of claims, occupier's liability claims, brought against the Health Service, dealt with by the Litigation Authority must be enormous. They should be familiar with dealing with these claims and appreciate the relevant issues.*

8. *The letter of 16th February, the first correspondence on the matter: "We refer to the above and previous correspondence. We have completed our investigations and confirm liability is denied. Our investigations have revealed that the Trust have no evidence of the incident occurring and therefore, put your client to strict proof that the incident occurred as alleged.*

Please note the Trust have no documents to disclose." In an occupier's liability case, of course, the Claimant clearly has to establish that the accident occurred as she alleges. She then has to also satisfy the Court that the occupier of the premises, in this case the Tameside Trust, have not taken such steps as were reasonable to provide for her safety whilst using the premises.

9. *Accordingly the issues which the Court would have to deal with were firstly, whether the accident occurred as claimed as a pure issue of fact and, of course, in relation to that the Defendant may have information in that the accident may have been witnessed by its staff. But often it will be the case that it has no direct evidence, in which case its entirely appropriate for it to say to the Claimant "well you prove that it happened". It is in relation to the second element that its response really was entirely unsatisfactory. The Litigation Authority must have been aware that once the Claimant had satisfied the Court that the accident had occurred as she alleged, it was then up to it to establish to the Court's satisfaction that it had a suitable system in place and the Court would clearly expect that system to be documented.*

10. *Under the Pre-action Protocol ("PAP") the Trust -- or the Litigation Authority on behalf of the Trust, was under a duty to set out, not on a fully pleaded basis but concisely, what its case was and in particular, was then under an obligation to provide documentation. That is dealt with in the rules under the Pre-action Protocol for PI claims and appears at page 2385 in the present White Book, paragraph 265:*

> ***"The Defendant should also enclose with the response, documents in their possession which are material to the issues between the parties, and which would be likely to be ordered to be disclosed by the Court, either on an application for pre-action disclosure, or on disclosure during proceedings."***

Clearly in any proceedings such as this claim the Court would have made an order for standard disclosure. Disclosure would have to be given of any documentation which set out the system and in particular, any records to confirm that the system was indeed being complied with. It is one thing to say we have this system, a piece of paper which says "this is what our system is", it is another thing for the Court to be satisfied that in fact that system is being properly implemented. The obligation was on the Defendants to provide at that early stage that documentation. This reflects the "cards on the table" ethos incorporated into the CPR to try and deal with issues at an early stage and avoid, whenever possible, litigation. It obviously would be somewhat burdensome for the Defendant. It would require somebody at the Trust to go through the documentation to pull out the appropriate pieces of paper. One would not have thought that it would be that difficult, but it was an obligation they were subject to. It is not here a case of the Defendant not dealing with disclosure. The Litigation Authority state in terms "we have no documents to disclose". That, perhaps not unreasonably, was taken by the Claimant's solicitors as an indication, somewhat unbelievably, that in the Defendant did not have any systems, because otherwise they would clearly have documentation to disclose. Had the

Defendant failed to address the issue of documentation the Claimant would have probably issued an application for pre action disclosure. Such an application was inappropriate because the Defendant's legal representative had said that the Defendant did not have any documents.

11. *So, proceedings were issued, a defence was then filed. The defence again put the Claimant to proof at paragraph 1, but goes on at paragraphs 2(a), 2(c) to set out that it has a proper systemin place. It says:*

At paragraph 2a "Relevant risk assessments have been performed prior to the Claimant's attendance at the Trust. The Defendant took such care as is reasonable to ensure the Claimant would be reasonably safe when attending the premises" and

At paragraph 2(b) "The Defendant employed contract cleaners to clean the area and regularly inspect it to ensure the floor was clean. In addition all employees are trained to look for and report any hazards."

So the Defendant is specifically pleading that they have a system in place for ensuring, as far as they can, that the premises are safe. It must be borne in mind that the obligation under the1957Actisnotab-solutebutistotakereasonablesteps. That was fully appreciated by the Claimant's solicitors, who were aware of the Ward v. Tesco decision and cited it repeatedly to the Defendant's representative.

12. The Court made the usual directions, including a direction for disclosure. The Defendant's first disclosure was made on 5th January 2016 in the usual form. It is important to appreciate that that form was signed -- one never knows who it is signed by because somewhat strangely this form does not mirror the statement of truth provisions which require the name of the signatory to be given, but it is signed on behalf of the Defendant and it states:

"I certify that I fully understand the duty of disclosure and to the best of my knowledge I have carried out that duty. I fully further certify that the list of documents set out in or attached to this form is a complete list of all documents which are or have been in my control and which I am obliged under the order to disclose."

In fact, all of the documents which are listed at page 10 are

ii. Trust assessments for slips, trips and falls: Trust's slips, trips and falls policy.

Standard cleaning schedule for Accident & Emergency."

So they are saying at that stage, not as they had said previously, "we have not got any documents," but they are saying, "we have documents and these are all the relevant documents" and there is a certificate to that effect signed by somebody on behalf of the Defendant.

13. ***What then happened is quite clear from the correspondence and documentation which I have been shown, that issues were raised by the Claimant's solicitors and they were then drip-fed further documentation, culminating in the disclosure at the end of February of 2016 of the crucial documentation, which was the Mitie documentation, Mitie being the cleaning contractor engaged by the Defendant to whom reference is made in paragraph 2 of the defence. The crucial documents are in fact documents 10 and 11, that is the Mitie cleaning rota for the year from week commencing 15th December 2014 and a copy of Mitie's daily work schedule for the A & E Department. That is the documentation upon which the Defendant is relying to say, not only that it has a proper system in place and has taken reasonable steps to ensure that visitors to its premises are safe, but also that that system is being implemented and is in operation. <u>That documentation should have all been supplied back at the beginning of the proceedings, before issue and clearly demon-</u>***

strates that the final paragraph of the Litigation Authority's letter of 16th February 2015 is, in pure and simple terms, false.

14. *What then happened was that after a further short flurry about photographs, the Claimant's solicitors reviewed the matter, took further instructions and then held discussions which resulted in the discontinuance of the claim, having reached the agreement with Weightmans which was recorded in the order made by me on 8th April.*

15. ***The Defendant's behaviours in the conduct of this litigation was entirely unacceptable. It's exactly the type of conduct which Part 44.2 is designed to address. Under the modern costs provisions, of course, the costs sanctions become increasingly important. The Claimant's solicitors are pursuing these matters, PI claims, and at the end of the claim are recovering costs which are fixed and which are not by any stretch of the imagination, generous. There is a danger of -- I am not saying it has happened in this case -- this is a pure inadequacy of approach by the Litigation Authority and the Trust, but there is a danger that defendants and their representatives will cause difficulties in the course of litigation, so as to run up the work which claimant's solicitors are having to do in the knowledge that those solicitors cannot recover costs reflecting that work. And of course, it always has to be borne in mind the provisions of CPR 1.3, that the parties to litigation have an obligation to assist the Court to further the overriding objective. The overriding objective firstly being to try and avoid costs and the issue of proceedings if at all possible, which is the whole purpose of the pre-action protocol, of course and secondly, when such claims are brought that they be dealt with in an efficient manner, in a proper manner so as to avoid excessive costs, involving public resources, delay and so on.***

16. *Various issues have arisen, the first is the question of evidence., Mr Smith makes the valid and very fair point that, strictly, there is no evidence that has been filed by the Claimant in support of his or her contention that the claim would have been abandoned at an*

early stage had the Defendants produced the documentation which they were under an obligation to produce. Clearly there should have been a statement by Ms Ireland that should have been in proper form and should have been provided. I do not have that. What I do have is a detailed skeleton argument prepared by Ms Ireland, which, whilst it does not bear her signature, does at the end bear her name and is clearly a document produced by her of which she is the author. It is not endorsed with a statement of truth, but of course, I have discretion under Rule 3.10 in relation to errors of procedure and so on and I am satisfied in the circumstance that it is appropriate for me to treat the factual content of that document as evidence. And I am satisfied on the balance of probabilities that had the NHS Litigation Authority produced under the PAP the documentation which they should have produced, i.e. the risk assessments and most crucially the Mitie documentation, then the claim would not have gone any further. There clearly was misconduct on the part of the Defendant.

17. *The matter does not rest there, however, because this is a fixed costs case and it is suggested by Mr Smith that it is a binary system and that you either get the fixed costs or none at all, the fixed costs for a settlement at that stage would have been £3,790. Issues of indemnity also arose, they were in fact raised by me, I set that particular hare running. But I have been referred to, I cannot remember whether it was High Court or Court of Appeal decision, which indicates that the indemnity principle does not apply in cases covered by the fixed costs regime.*

MR SMITH: It is Simon J, sir.

DISTRICT JUDGE SWINDLEY: Thank you.

18. I am satisfied that the provisions of Rule 44.2 can be applied. It would be a nonsensical situation if the rules which are provided by Rule 44.2 to give the Court the power to impose sanctions to penalise those who abuse the system, and clearly there has been abuse here by the Trust and possibly by the Litigation Authority initially representing them. I am certainly not suggesting that

Weightmans have been dealing with it improperly, they are obviously having to deal with what information they are supplied. But it would be a nonsensical situation if the rules, in an appropriate case where the fixed costs regime did apply, precluded the Court from imposing the sanctions provided under Rule 44.2 and 44.2, of course, gives the Court an unqualified discretion. I do not accept that I am bound by the Part 45 scales, but I clearly have to bear them in mind. It would be nonsensical if the Claimant's solicitors could achieve a windfall and recover more costs than they would have done had the matter gone to trial or settled in favour of the Claimant at the stage that it was discontinued. That would be absolutely nonsensical.

19. *The approach taken by Ms Ireland in her submission as to costs seems to me entirely appropriate. What she basically says is, had we been successful we would have been awarded our base costs(that is the costs without the added 20% of damages) which at that stage were £3,790, but had we not proceeded after we had been supplied with the appropriate documentation by the Trust Litigation Authority, we had already incurred some costs, the scale figure for those would be £950 and the accordingly the appropriate way of dealing with it is to set one against the other and award the Claimant's solicitors £2,840 plus VAT. I am satisfied that is an appropriate way of dealing with the matter and I award that sum, plus the fee for Mr Ballin's report at £426, which I calculate to be a total of £3,834. In relation to the various costs or the Court fees rather, I see that Scott Rees have already written to the Court sending the forms completed by their client to get a return of the fees, she apparently being someone who was exempt from the payment of fees.*

20. *Accordingly, I make an order in favour of the Claimant for £3,834.*

<u>BROADHURST v TAN (2016)</u> was an important case which set out the principle that in a fixed costs personal injury claims governed by CPR 45, costs were payable on the indemnity basis, where a party had

made a Part 36 basis and then beaten this offer at Trial. The Court said in Broadhurst:-

A new rule 36.14A was also introduced to prescribe the costs consequences following judgment in section IIIA cases. While it modified some aspects of rule 36.14 (which set out the cost consequences following judgment) in fixed costs cases, it left rule 36.14(3) unmodified. Rule 36.14 provided, so far as material:

"36.14 – Costs consequences following judgment

(1)... (3)

Subject to rule 36.14A, this rule applies where upon judgment being entered...

(b) judgment against the defendant is at least as advantageous to the claimant as the proposals contained in a claimant's part 36 offer.

Subject to paragraph (6), where rule 36.14(1)(b) applies, the court will, unless it considers it unjust to do so, order that the claimant is entitled to –

(a) interest on the whole or part of any sum of money (excluding interest) awarded at a rate not exceeding 10% above base rate for some or all of the period starting with the date on which the relevant period expired;

(b) costs on the indemnity basis from the date on which the relevant period expired;

(c) interest on those costs at a rate not exceeding 10% above base rate and

(d) an additional amount, which shall not exceed £75,000, calculated by applying the prescribed percentage set out below..."

10. Rule 36.14A provided, so far as material:

"36.14A – Costs consequences following judgment where Section IIIA of Part 45 applies

Where a claim no longer continues under the RTA or EL/PL Protocol pursuant to rule 45.29A(1), rule 36.14 applies with the following modifications.

Subject to paragraphs (3),(3A) and (3B) where an order for costs is made pursuant to rule 36.14(2)-

(a) the claimant will be entitled to the fixed costs in Table 6B, 6C or 6D in section IIIA of Part 45 for the stage applicable at the date on which the relevant period expired; and

(b) the claimant will be liable for the defendant's costs from the date on which the relevant period expired to the date of the judgment.

Subject to paragraphs (3A) and (3B) where the claimant fails to obtain a judgment more advantageous than the defendant's Protocol offer -

(a) the claimant will be entitled to the applicable Stage 1 and Stage 2 fixed costs in Table 6 or Table 6A in Section III of Part 45; and

(b) the claimant will be liable for the defendant's costs from the date on which the Protocol offer is deemed to be made to the date of judgment; and

Fixed costs shall be calculated by reference to the amount which is awarded.

Where the court makes an order for costs in favour of the defendant –

(a) *the court will have regard to; and*

(b) *the amount of costs ordered shall not exceed,*

the fixed costs in Table 6B, 6C or 6D in Section IIIA of Part 45 applicable at the date of judgment, less the fixed costs to which the claimant is entitled under paragraph (2) or (3).

The parties are entitled to disbursements allowed in accordance with rule 45.29I incurred in any period for which costs are payable to them."

"I would allow the appeal in the case of Broadhurst and dismiss the appeal in the case of Smith largely for the reasons stated by Mr Williams.

If rule 45.29B stood alone, then subject to various rules in Part 45 which are immaterial, the only costs allowable in a section IIIA case to a claimant who was awarded costs following judgment in his favour would be "(a) the fixed costs in rule 45.29C and (b) disbursements in accordance with rule 45.29I". But rule 45.29B does not stand alone. The need to take account of Part 36 offers in section IIIA cases was recognised by the draftsman of the rules. Indeed, rule 36.14A is headed "costs consequences following judgment where section IIIA of Part 45 applies". Rule 45.29F (8) provides that, where a Part 36 offer is accepted in a section IIIA case, "rule 36.10A will apply instead of this rule". And rule 45.29F(9) provides that, where in such a case upon judgment being entered the claimant fails to obtain a judgment more advantageous than the claimant's Part 36 offer, "rule 36.14A will apply instead of this rule". Rule 45.29F does not, however, make provision as to what should happen where the claimant makes a successful Part 36 offer.

Mr Laughland submits that, since rule 45.29F makes no such provision, the basic or general rule in rule 45.29B that the only costs allowable are fixed costs and disbursements carries the day. But that is to ignore rule 36.14A which is headed "Costs consequences following judgment where section IIIA of Part 45 applies". Rule 36.14A(1) provides that in a section IIIA case "rule 36.14 applies with the following modifications". As we have seen, rule 36.14(3) provides that, where a claimant makes a successful Part 36 offer, the court will, unless it considers it unjust to do so, order that the claimant is entitled to four enhanced benefits including "(b) his costs on the indemnity basis from the date on which the relevant period expired".

The effect of rules 36.14 and 36.14A when read together is that, where a claimant makes a successful Part 36 offer, he is entitled to costs assessed on the indemnity basis. Thus, rule 36.14 is modified only to the extent stated by 36.14A. Since rule 36.14(3) has not been modified by rule 36.14A, it continues to have full force and effect. The tension between rule 45.29B and rule 36.14A must, therefore, be resolved in favour of rule 36.14A. I reach this conclusion as a straightforward matter of interpretation and without recourse to the canon of construction that, where there is a conflict between a specific provision and a general provision, the former takes precedence. As we have seen, there is disagreement as to which is the relevant general provision in the present context. Mr Williams submits that it is rule 36.14; and Mr Laughland submits that it is rule 45.29B. I do not find it necessary to resolve this difference.

Rule 36.14A(8) provides further support for my conclusion. This provision states that in a section IIIA case the parties (i.e. claimant as well as defendant) are entitled to disbursements allowed in accordance with rule 45.29I in any period for which costs are payable to them. This reflects rule 45.29B(b). If, as Mr Laughland contends, rule 45.29B prevailed over rule 36.14A in any event, this provision would have been unnecessary. It is significant that rule 36.14A does not contain a provision which reflects rule 45.29B(a) and 45.29C. In my view, the fact that rule 36.14A contains provision for payment of disbursements in accordance with rule 45.29B(b), but not for payment of fixed costs in accordance with rule 45.29B(a) confirms that the interpretation that I have adopted above is correct.

I find yet further support for the conclusion that I have reached in the wider contextual points made by Mr Williams to which I have referred at para 13 above which it is unnecessary to repeat.

For all these reasons, I do not consider that there is any doubt as to the true meaning of these rules. The tension is clearly resolved in favour of rule 36.14A. If that were wrong, then it would be legitimate to use the Explanatory Memorandum as an aid to construction (this was not the Explanatory Note to the statutory instrument). That is because the three conditions specified by Lord Browne-Wilkinson in Pepper v Hart [1993] AC 593 would be satisfied. First, the rules would, in material part, be obscure and/or ambiguous. Secondly, the Explanatory Memorandum was prepared by the Ministry of Justice (the promoter of the rules) and was laid before Parliament together with the 2013 Amendment Rules. I can see no difference in principle between a statement made in Parliament by a Minister or other promotor of a Bill and an explanatory memorandum laid before Parliament by the promotor of rules. The Rules are subject to the negative resolution procedure. Parliament has no power to amend the Rules, but could have annulled them if it had wished to do so. Thirdly, the statement in the Explanatory Memorandum relied on by the claimants is clear on the issue which arises on this appeal".

The Jackson report does propose change to the *Broadhurst* rules and says:-

Broadhurst v Tan and the effect of an order for indemnity costs. The one issue which cannot be ducked, however, is Broadhurst v Tan [2016] EWCA Civ 94; [2016] 1 WLR 1928. This decision, unless its effect is modified by rule change, will impact upon fixed costs generally. This issue is equally important in relation to higher value claims, but I deal with it here and will not repeat the discussion in later chapters. Views on this issue are sharply divided:

(i) Nine of my assessors consider that, although CPR Part 36 must continue to bring rewards for claimants who make effective Part 36 offers, in the context of a fixed costs regime it would be better for there to be a percentage uplift on the fixed costs rather than an order for indemnity costs. This will avoid the need for a detailed assessment of costs. Also, it will provide certainty for litigants. Certainty is an essential feature of an FRC regime. As to the level of percentage uplift, views range between 25% and 50%.

(ii) Five of my assessors take the opposite view. Nicholas Bacon QC writes:

"I do not agree with the proposal that we do away with the Broadhurst indemnity costs order. These cases on indemnity costs are not clogging up the courts with detailed assessments. It is a powerful message for a party to consider rejection/acceptance. A 30% enhancement is not sufficient to redress the failure to accept an offer. It ignores the fact that as between solicitor and client more than the fixed costs will have been incurred by the client. Why should a client not be entitled to be reimbursed for their actual legal spend, rather than fixed costs, where a party has misconducted themselves or caused a party to incur costs unnecessarily because an earlier offer should have been accepted."

I have set out the competing arguments, because this is the only issue on which my assessors are sharply divided. After considering the powerful arguments on both sides, on balance, for the reasons set out in sub-paragraph (i) above, I favour replacing indemnity costs with a percentage uplift of 30% or perhaps 40%. BUT this is a clear issue of policy, which will need to be addressed in the consultation exercise following this report".

Sharp v Leeds City Council – PAD application costs

Sharp held that the fixed costs regime applicable to the Pre-action Protocol for Low Value Personal Injury (Employers' Liability and Public Liability) Claims applied to the costs of an application for pre-action disclosure by a claimant even where the claim had started off under the protocol but was no longer continuing under it when the application was made. However the Court said that the fixed costs regime could be disapplied where there was unreasonable behavior:-

38. *But in my judgment the answer to this submission lies not in subjecting the fixed costs regime to an implied exception for PAD applications which exposed recalcitrant defendants to an altogether higher but variable level of recoverable costs liability, to be determined by assessment. Rather, the answer lies in the availability of an application under Part 45.29J, if exceptional circumstances can be*

shown or, for the future, in a recognition by the Rule Committee that the fixed costs regime needs to be kept under review, and defects in it remedied by adjustment of the fixed allowances where that can be shown to be justified.

39. *It may well be that the frequency with which defendants fail to comply with their Protocol disclosure obligations may make it difficult to pass the exceptional circumstances hurdle in Part 45.29J, although I would not regard deliberate disregard of those obligations as unexceptional merely because it was frequently encountered. It may be that the very limited recovery of expenditure on a PAD application under the fixed costs regime means that such applications are not as effective as a means of sanctioning breach of Protocol disclosure obligations as they should be. If that is made good by appropriate evidence, then it seems to me that some consideration by way of review to the establishment of a more generous, but still fixed, recovery of costs of such applications would be justified.*

40. *By contrast, to throw open PAD applications generally to the recovery of assessed costs would in my view be to risk giving rise to an undesirable form of satellite litigation in which there would be likely to be incentives for the incurring of disproportionate expense, which is precisely what the fixed costs regime, viewed as a whole, is designed to avoid. The fixed costs regime inevitably contains swings and roundabouts, and lawyers who assist claimants by participating in it are accustomed to taking the rough with the smooth, in pursuing legal business which is profitable overall.*

Bird v Acorn (2017) – a disposal hearing was a "trial" where a personal injury claim had started under the Pre-Action Protocol for Low Value Personal Injury (Employers Liability and Public Liability) Claims and had settled after judgment but before trial. Consequently, the correct scale of fixed costs was contained in the third column of part B of Table 6D. The Court said:-

22. *Finally, there are passages in Jackson LJ's Interim Report, in particular at paragraph 1.12 and following in chapter 22, which*

suggest that the three columns in what is now Table 6D part B were intended usually to be steps in a ladder. But those general observations do not detract from the interpretation of the definition of trial at which I have arrived. In every case where a claimant obtains judgment for damages to be assessed, followed by a disposal hearing for that assessment, there will be a progression from column 1 (which comes into force when proceedings are issued) to column 3, when the disposal hearing is listed. The fact that column 2 is jumped over because there is no intermediate allocation to the fast track seems to me to be just one of those events which means that the three columns will not always be triggered in succession. But that by no means undermines the good sense of a conclusion that, once there has been a listing for a disposal hearing, column 3 is triggered.

CHAPTER THREE
OL/PL – UPDATES, CASES AND KEY DECISIONS

1984 Occupiers Act

SLAWOMIR KOLASA v EALING HOSPITAL NHS TRUST (2015) – A hospital trust did not owe a duty of care under the 1984 Act to an intoxicated patient who had discharged himself and sustained injuries after climbing over a wall on a ramp outside the hospital and falling 30 feet to the ground. The danger of the drop was obvious at all times, the wall was of sufficient height and maintenance, and the trust was not obliged to provide further protection. The Judgment said:-

> 36. *Before I turn to the legal principles which govern this case and the submissions of learned counsel I should indicate that in this case I am not considering any duty of care which might be argued to have been owed to the Claimant by the Defendant as a patient brought to the hospital in an ambulance. He had voluntarily discharged himself from A&E and, rightly, Particulars of Negligence and/or Breach of Statutory Duty (g) to (j) inclusive were struck out of the Particulars of Claim, leaving this a claim purely under the Occupiers' Liability Acts, to which duties the pleading of negligence adds nothing.*
>
> 42. *I also make the finding of fact that, although when the Claimant was brought to the hospital and was put to wait in A&E he was a visitor to the hospital and was owed the common duty of care under section 2(2) of the 1957 Act, his act of climbing over the wall was not an act covered by his general permission to be on the site as a patient nor was it part of the permission given by the Defendant to patients leaving the site after, or even without, treatment. He was, therefore, no longer an invitee or visitor but a trespasser.*
>
> 43. ***To use the famous example of Lord Justice Scrutton in The Calgarth [1927] P 93 at page 110:***

> ***"When you invite a person into your house to use the staircase, you do not invite him to slide down the banisters – you invite him to use the staircase in the ordinary way in which it is used."***

44. ***Mr. Norris' primary submission to me is that the protection extended both to visitors and to trespassers under the 1957 and 1984 Acts respectively is from danger caused by the state of the premises, an "occupancy duty" rather than a more general obligation to protect the visitor/trespasser from danger he may face while on the premises.*** *That is clear from the discussion of the law at paragraph 12-04 of the current edition of Clerk and Lindsell on Torts. I accept that submission.*

45. ***The most helpful authority which has been cited to me is the Court of Appeal decision in Keown v Coventry Healthcare NHS Trust [2006] 1 WLR 953.*** *That case establishes or re-establishes the principle I have just referred to. The Claimant in that case was an 11 year old child who climbed the underside of an external metal fire escape of an accommodation block and day clinic in the grounds of a hospital owned by the Defendant trust and fell from a height of about 30 feet severely injuring himself. There was evidence in that case that the hospital grounds were known as a place where children liked to play. The claim was brought under the 1984 Act on the basis that the fire escape constituted a material danger and allurement to children. The Claimant accepted he appreciated that climbing the underside of the fire escape was dangerous and that he should not be doing it. The first instance judge found the occupier Defendant one third to blame for the accident as they were aware that children might come on to the staircase. The headnote sufficiently summarises the ratio of the case:*

> *"Held, allowing the appeal, that the threshold requirement posed by section 1(1)(a) of the Occupiers' Liability Act 1984 was not whether there was a risk of suffering injury by reason of the state of the premises, but whether there was a risk of injury by reason of any danger due to the state of the premises;*

> *that a fire escape was not inherently dangerous, so that, if a person chose to create danger by climbing it improperly knowing that it was dangerous to do so, any danger was due to such person's activity and not the state of the premises; that, in general, the age of the trespasser was not relevant, but it was a question of fact and degree whether premises which were not dangerous from the point of view of an adult could be dangerous for a child; that the Claimant had been aware not only that there was a risk of falling but also that his actions were dangerous and he should not have been climbing the exterior of the fire escape; and that, accordingly, no risk arose out of the state of the fire escape there being no element of disrepair or structural deficiency"*

46. *While every case turns on its own facts, the Claimant's case here is actually far weaker than that of the Claimant in Keown.* ***In my judgment, there was nothing dangerous about the state of the premises where the Claimant fell.*** *The wall was of an adequate, safe height. It was no lower than walls at the sides of bridges or piers. The provision of an additional rail after Mr Talbot's accident was the reaction of a risk averse Defendant to the circumstances of his particular accident, which involved someone sitting on a part of the first floor perimeter wall in an area known to be used for recreational purposes, and, thus, falling to his death. The Defendant acted on the specific recommendation of the Safetymark report that the additional railing would deter people sitting on the wall. In my judgment, they could not have been criticised for not erecting the rail. The risk of falling when sitting on the wall was very obvious, whether by day or night. Neither rail nor warning signs were necessary to alert adults or even children to the risk. The report does not evidence that the wall and drop should have been protected or that they were unsafe. They were not. What was unsafe was the activity of sitting on the wall, an activity that Mr Krajewski had sensibly warned several people about prior to Mr Kolasa's accident.*

47. *However, that warning or even the knowledge which I find it can be inferred that the Defendant had of people sitting on the wall,*

does not evidence that the wall and drop represented an inherent danger either visitors or trespassers. It was not a hidden trap. It was easily visible and the danger of the drop obvious by day or night. It was not in a position in which it presented a danger. It was not in a defective state. It did not need guarding.

48. *In any event, the railing which the Defendant erected after Mr Talbot's accident, and because of that accident and the report's recommendations, was erected to deter sitting on the wall and not climbing over the wall. The railing would not have prevented what the Claimant did, namely to climb over the wall. What was dangerous was not the state of the premises but what the Claimant, an adult, who had voluntarily consumed far too much alcohol and who was drunk, actually did. In truth, this accident was nothing to do with the state of the premises and was, instead, the entire fault of the Claimant, sad though it is to say that, given his very serious injuries.*

49. *In many ways that decides the case against the Claimant, but in deference to the arguments of both counsel I should consider other legal issues.*

50. *In the absence of a supervisory duty to the Claimant, as a person who had been attending the hospital for treatment but had discharged himself before he could be seen, and having regard to the deletion of particulars based on a supervisory duty, it matters not that the Defendant could have expected that people who might be drunk and even those who might be in a shocked or upset state due to injury, might be present in or around A&E. The Defendant had not accepted, nor was it under, any duty to take particular care of a drunken adult. There is no satisfactory evidence that the Claimant was in fact suffering from the continuing effects of a head injury, even though there is some very slight evidence he had been concussed.*

51. ***It should be noted that, if the Claimant had been a visitor, section 2 (2) of the 1957 Act imposed on the Defendant a duty to take such care as in all the circumstances of the case was reasonable to see that he would be reasonably safe for the purposes for***

which he was invited or permitted by the occupier to be there. *Those purposes did not include climbing over the wall and I am wholly satisfied that the Defendant did discharge that duty if the Claimant was a visitor.*

52. *However, as I have found above, he was not a visitor at the time of the accident, he was a trespasser because he had gone further than his implied invitation and had tried to climb the wall.* ***Thus I have to consider the 1984 Act. The relevant provisions of the Act are as follows:***

> *"(1) The rules enacted by this section shall have effect, in place of the rules of the common law, to determine—*
>
> *(a) whether any duty is owed by a person as occupier of premises to persons other than his visitors in respect of any risk of their suffering injury on the premises by reason of any danger due to the state of the premises or to things done or omitted to be done on them; and*
>
> *(b) if so, what that duty is...............*
>
> *(3) An occupier of premises owes a duty to another (not being his visitor) in respect of any such risk as is referred to in sub-section (1) above if—*
>
> *(a) he is aware of the danger or has reasonable grounds to believe that it exists;*
>
> *(b) he knows or has reasonable grounds to believe that the other is in the vicinity of the danger concerned or that he may come into the vicinity of the danger (in either case, whether the other has lawful authority for being in that vicinity or not); and*
>
> *(c) the risk is one against which, in all the circumstances of the case, he may reasonably be expected to offer the other some pro-tection.*

(4) Where, by virtue of this section, an occupier of premises owes a duty to another in respect of such a risk, the duty is to take such care as is reasonable in all the circumstances of the case to see that he does not suffer injury on the premises by reason of the danger concerned.

(5) Any duty owed by virtue of this section in respect of a risk may, in an appropriate case, be discharged by taking such steps as are reasonable in all the circumstances of the case to give warning of the danger concerned or to discourage persons from incurring the risk.

(6) No duty is owed by virtue of this section to any person in respect of risks willingly accepted as his by that person (the question whether a risk was so accepted to be decided on the same principles as in other cases in which one person owes a duty of care to another)."

53. ***Applying those provisions sequentially, as I have already determined, there was no danger due to the state of the premises and there was nothing done or omitted to be done in relation to the wall that made it dangerous.***

54. *Although the Defendant was aware of people climbing on to the perimeter wall and sitting on it, that was not the risk presented in this accident. Mr Levene submitted that I should not be too "nit picking" in relation to the designation or description of the "risk" presented and known to the Defendant, but the risk of someone climbing over the wall was of an entirely different nature and the Defendant was not and had no reason to be aware of the existence of that risk.*

55. *That remains the case, in my judgment, despite the fact that subsequent to the Claimant's accident the Defendant erected the metal rails.* ***In Tomlinson v Congleton Borough Council and another [2002] EWCA Civ 309, the Defendant was aware of an increased risk of an accident from the unauthorised use of the lake*** *and had begun work on a plan to landscape the shores and plant over*

the beaches from which people swam. That action did not evidence that the premises were not reasonably safe under the 1984 or 1957 Acts before the work was started.

56. *In any event, if climbing over the wall and/or falling from it were the risks concerned and there had been evidence that the Defendant either was aware of them (which it was not) or had reasonable grounds to believe that they existed (which they did not),* ***then they were not risks against which, in all the circumstances of the case, it might reasonably be expected to offer the Claimant some additional protection.*** *I accept Mr Levene's submission that A&E departments do have drunken people attending them and people with head injuries, but in all the circumstances no further protection than the wall itself, which was of an adequate height, needed to be provided. It was entirely reasonable for the Defendant to have concentrated on the risk actually known to them when it was brought to their attention, namely, the sitting on the wall by certain visitors.*

57. *Thus, in my judgment, the Claimant has not established that the Defendant owed him a duty of care under the 1984 Act in relation to the risk of his climbing over the wall and falling to the area below. If he had established that they did then I would have concluded that they had taken such care as was reasonable in all the circumstances to see he did not suffer injury on the premises by reason of the danger presented by wall and drop.* ***It would have been going further than was reasonable to raise the height of the wall or put a rail or some other deterrent on top of the wall and it would not have been effective in this case.***

58. ***There was no need to give a warning because the risk was obvious.***

59. *Finally, although the Claimant was drunk and had sustained some head or facial injury that evening, I am satisfied he willingly accepted the risk of climbing over the*

wall, though of course it was something he would not have done had he been sober. Thus by reason of section 1 (6) no duty would be owed by the Defendant to him.

60. *It seems to me to be quite obvious that, at the time of the accident, the Claimant was a trespasser or, phrasing it alternatively, was no longer a visitor acting within the scope of his permission but, if I were wrong about that,* ***then I am entirely satisfied that the Defendant had discharged the common duty of care to the Claimant under section 2(2) of the 1957 Act by building and maintaining a perimeter wall of sufficient height and adequately lighting the area around the A&E.***

61. *Mr Norris also argues that the deliberate actions of the Claimant were the entire cause of the accident. As I have already indicated, I consider that is entirely correct and the Claimant would fail on that basis as well. That seems to me a more appropriate way of putting the matter than to say that this is a case where the Claimant is 100% contributorily negligent.*

62. *For the reasons I have given, therefore, I dismiss the Claimant's claim.*

Key Points

1. The protection extended both to visitors and to trespassers under the 1957 and 1984 Acts respectively is from danger caused by the state of the premises, an "occupancy duty" rather than a more general obligation to protect the visitor/trespasser from danger he may face while on the premises.

2. In order to establish breach- there must be something dangerous about the area in which the claimant was injured.

3. There is no need to provide a warning if the risk was obvious.

4. There needs to be danger due to the state of the premises and / or something that was done or omitted to be done in relation to make it dangerous.

5. There need to be a risk against which, in all the circumstances of the case, it might reasonably be expected to offer the Claimant some additional protection.

6. In *Tomlinson v Congleton Borough Council* and another [2002] EWCA Civ 309, the Defendant was aware of an increased risk of an accident from the unauthorised use of the lake.

Highways Act 1980

PAUL SINGH v CITY OF CARDIFF COUNCIL (2017) looked at a claim both under the Highways Act section 41 and Occupiers Act section 2. The accident had not been caused by a breach of a duty under the Highways Act 1980 s.41, the Occupiers' Liability Act 1957 s.2 or breach of a common law duty.

The Court said went through the key principles of a Highways Act claim and said:-

> 1. *This is a claim for damages arising out of an incident on land between Fishguard Road and Trenchard Drive, Llanishen in Cardiff. The claimant, Mr Paul Singh, was walking home in the early hours of 10 December 2011 along a path that lead to a foot-bridge over Llanishen Brook. At some stage, he ceased to be on the path and went down into Llanishen Brook. He remained in the brook overnight and was found the following morning. He sustained severe injuries. He claims that the injuries were caused (1) by a breach of a duty owed by the defendant, Cardiff City Council, under section 41 of the Highways Act 1980 ("the 1980 Act") to maintain the footpath (2) a breach of the duty owed by the defendant under section 2 of the Occupier's Liability Act 1957 ("the 1957 Act") or*

(3) common law negligence on the part of the defendant. The defendant denies liability.

THE FIRST ISSUE – THE 1980 ACT

30 Mr Jones, on behalf of the claimant, submits that this footpath is a highway maintainable at public expense and this is accepted by the defendant. Mr Jones submits that the unevenness of the surface of the footpath and the irregularity of the concrete edging units gave rise to an state of disrepair and so as to amount to an actionable defect which, he submitted, caused the claimant to slip off the path and led to his injuries.

The Legal Framework

31 Section 41 of the 1980 Act provides, so far as material, as that:

> ***"41.— Duty to maintain highways maintainable at public expense.***
>
> ***"(1) The authority who are for the time being the highway authority for a highway maintainable at the public expense are under a duty, subject to subsections (2) and (4) below, to maintain the highway.***
>
> ***Judgment Approved by the court for handing down. Singh v City of Cardiff Council***
>
> ***"(1A) In particular, a highway authority are under a duty to ensure, so far as is reasonably practicable, that safe passage along a highway is not endangered by snow or ice."***

32 Section 329 of the 1980 Act provides that:

> ***"maintenance" includes repair, and "maintain" and "maintainable" are to be construed accordingly".***

33 Section 58 of the provides for a special defence. That section provides that:

> *"58.— Special defence in action against a highway authority for damages for non- repair of highway.*
>
> *"(1) In an action against a highway authority in respect of damage resulting from their failure to maintain a highway maintainable at the public expense it is a defence (without prejudice to any other defence or the application of the law relating to contributory negligence) to prove that the authority had taken such care as in all the circumstances was reasonably required to secure that the part of the highway to which the action relates was not dangerous for traffic.*
>
> *"(2) For the purposes of a defence under subsection (1) above, the court shall in particular have regard to the following matters:—*
>
> *(a) the character of the highway, and the traffic which was reasonably to be expected to use it;*
>
> *(b) the standard of maintenance appropriate for a highway of that character and used by such traffic;*
>
> *(c) the state of repair in which a reasonable person would have expected to find the highway;*
>
> *(d) whether the highway authority knew, or could reasonably have been expected to know, that the condition of the part of the highway to which the action relates was likely to cause danger to users of the highway;*
>
> *(e) where the highway authority could not reasonably have been expected to repair that part of the highway before the cause of action arose, what warning notices of its condition had been displayed;*
>
> *but for the purposes of such a defence it is not relevant to prove that the highway authority had arranged for a competent*

> *person to carry out or supervise the maintenance of the part of the highway to which the action relates unless it is also proved that the authority had given him proper instructions with regard to the maintenance of the highway and that he had carried out the instructions."*

34 ***The claimant must establish that there is a breach and that that breach caused injury of a type which the statute intended to prevent.*** *If he does that, the defendant will have a defence to the claim if it can establish the defence established in section 58 of the 1980 Act.*

35 In terms of the scope of the duty imposed by section 41 of the 1980 Act, the Court of Appeal held in Jones v Rhondda Cynon Taff CBC [2008] EWCA Civ 1497, [2990] R.T.R. 13 at paragraph 11 that it is an absolute duty in the sense that:

> *Judgment Approved by the court for handing down. Singh v City of Cardiff Council*
>
> ***"the highway has to be maintained in a state of repair that it is reasonably passable for the ordinary traffic of the neighbourhood without danger caused by its physical condition".***

36 In James v Preseli Pembrokeshire District Council [1999] P.I.Q.R. 114, Lloyd L.J. held that:

> ***"The question in each case is whether the particular spot where the plaintiff tripped or fell was dangerous. If it was, then the defendant authority concedes that there was a failure to maintain the highway and the plaintiff would be entitled to recover. But if the particular spot was not dangerous, then it is irrelevant that there were other spots nearby that were dangerous or that the area as a whole was due for resurfacing.***

"This point was made crystal-clear by the decision of this court in Whitworth v. The Mayor, Aldermen and Burgesses of The City of Manchester . In that case the decision in favour of the plaintiff had been founded on the ground that the pavement as a whole was in poor condition. The Court of Appeal rejected that approach. Russell L.J. said at page 6 of the transcript dated June 17, 1971: "The relevant question is whether that which caused the accident constituted a danger, not whether nearby differences in levels which did not contribute to the accident constituted a danger."

"Edmund Davies L.J. said at page 7:

"What is quite clear is that ***when a plaintiff in a trip case claims that she fell by reason of the dangerous condition of the pavement, she must indicate where and how she fell and she must prove it; and it is then for the court to consider whether the place where she fell constituted a danger for which the local authority could properly be held liable."***

37 *Ralph Gibson L.J, who agreed with Lloyd L.J., observed that:*

"it has been established by the decisions of this court that the standard of care imposed by the law upon highway authorities is not to remove or repair all and any defects arising from failure to maintain, such as differences in level or gaps between paving stones, which might foreseeably cause a person using the carriageway or footpath to fall and suffer injury, but only those which are properly to be characterised as causing danger to pedestrians. There is, I think, an apparent element of circularity in some of the formulations of duty or breach of duty which have been advanced. Thus the test of dangerousness is one of reasonable foresight of harm to users of the highway. But in drawing the inference of dangerousness the court must not set too high a standard. Any defect, if its uncorrected presence is to impose a liability, must therefore be such that failure to repair shows a breach of duty. The escape from any apparent

> *circularity was stated, or re-stated, I think, by Steyn L.J. in Mills v Barnsley Metropolitan Borough Council [1992] P.I.Q.R. P291 (to which my Lord has already referred) where, in holding that no breach of duty had been established, he pointed to the fact that the risk of injury from the demonstrated defect was of a low order and that the fall suffered by the claimant in that case must have been caused by her inattention when passing over an uneven surface or by misfortune."*

The Present Case

38 First, and foremost, in the present case, in my judgment, any alleged defect in the highway did not, in fact, cause the injury that the claimant suffered. As I have found above, the claimant did not trip over the concrete edging units of the footpath nor did he slip on the depression in the footpath. He voluntarily stepped off the footpath onto the ground adjacent to, but not part of, the highway. He lost his footing on that ground and fell on to his back and then slid down the steep slope and into the brook. His claim for breach of the duty imposed by the 1980 Act fails, therefore, because the injury suffered was not caused by any alleged defect in the footpath.

39. *Secondly, and separately, I have considered whether the footpath at the location where the incident occurred was in a state of disrepair such as to amount to an actionable defect for the purposes of section 41 of the 1980 Act. I bear in mind that this footpath is approximately two meters wide. It has a metalled surface. It is well used as a means of going from one housing estate to another. It is used hundreds of times a day, and thousands of times a week, by people crossing over the brook.*

40. *The first defect identified and relied upon by the claimant is the broken and uneven edging units (there is an edging unit missing but that unit is missing near the bridge itself and not where the incident occurred). I find that the broken and uneven edging units are not such as to amount to a state of disrepair giving rise to a breach of the*

duty imposed by section 41 of the 1980 Act. The footpath is wide. There is ample room for persons to pass, and repass, over the footbridge without stepping on the concrete edging units. The risk of anyone tripping over the edging units at that point on the footpath and falling down into the brook is very low.

41. *That view is reinforced by the expert evidence. Mr Hopwood for the defendant gave evidence that the primary purpose of the edging units would be to support the footpath and they would not expect to be walked on. The footpath was wide enough to be used without there being any need to step on the edging units and to allow people to pass each other. Mr Runacres for the claimant did identify this as a defect. He was, however, primarily concerned in his evidence, in my judgment, with the risk arising at a later point on the footpath, namely the risk that if someone left the footpath they could fall over the wing wall or the retaining wall and have a vertical drop into the brook. He was concerned that persons could stumble and fall, or there was a risk of inadvertent access to the area where the walls were and where there would be a steep fall into the brook. He was less concerned with the risk posed by the edging units further back from the bridge where a person, if they stumbled on that edging unit, would stumble and fall onto soil. He considered that gave rise to a reduced risk. In my judgment, the broken and uneven edging units in the vicinity where the incident occurred were not in such a state of disrepair as to give rise to a breach of the section 41 duty.*

42. *The second defect identified is the depression caused, probably by the support subsiding and the surface of the footpath becoming uneven. This was described as a depression and was measured by Mr Hopwood as being a depression of 60 millimetres (although it is likely to have been less at the time of the incident). I accept the accuracy of his measurement. This matter is of more concern. It occurs on a well used metalled footpath used many hundreds of times a day. The evidence of Mr Hopwood is that any depression of over 40 millimetres would be a matter of concern, although he would regard it as low risk.*

43. On balance, I am satisfied that the depression did not amount to a defect or state of disrepair such as to cause a danger to pedestrians and its non-repair did not amount to a breach of section 41 of the 1980 Act. I accept that this is a busy footpath used many times a day. The depression, however, was not a pothole or a hazard capable of tripping someone. It was a change in height over an area to the left of the footpath. In terms of the location and the risk if a person did fall or slip from the path due to the depression, the person would fall onto soil adjacent to the area of the footpath containing the depression. There was no risk that the depression would cause someone to fall or stumble in such a way as to cause that person to fall over the wing wall or the retaining wall and endure a vertical drop into the brook. The risk posed by the depression was, therefore, relatively low as Mr Hopwood said.

44. *On balance, therefore, I consider that the presence of this depression on the footpath did not constitute a breach of the section 41 duty. I am reinforced in that conclusion by the fact that there is no record of any accident having occurred at this location over the time it is likely that a depression of something in the region of the size of this depression would have been present on the footpath. The claimant and Mr and Ms Donnelly who lived on the estates had used the footpath many times and not suffered an injury or had any cause to complain about the state of the footpath (Mr and Ms Donnelly had complained about the lights not working). The defendant provided the disclosure sought of complaints for three months from 1st October 2011 to 29 December 2011 and no complaints were recorded. Ms Bolwell made a witness statement stating that there had never been any complaints about the footbridge or the footpath before. Ms Bolwell was not well enough to give evidence and her evidence was not therefore tested in cross-examination. All the evidence is, however, that persons used the footpath hundreds of times a day when the depression was present and there was no recorded accident (still less a serious accident of the kind suffered by the claimant) and no recorded complaints. My conclusion that there is no breach of the section 41 duty is not dependent on the absence of*

recorded accidents or complaints: but it reinforces the conclusion that I have reached.

45. *For completeness, I mention the evidence of certain of the other witnesses. Mr Rowlands, a lands service officer at the parks department of the defendant, carried out a survey of a section of Llanishen Brook on 23 November 2011, shortly before the incident. He surveyed the brook from the Rugby Club to the footbridge. He marked the condition of the bridge as 2 on a scale of 1 to 5, 1 being poor and 5 being good. He explained in evidence that he based that remark on the appearance of the bridge, graffiti and the presence of a shopping trolley. He was not, he said, expressing a view on the safety of the footbridge. He also marked the condition of footways and walkways and marked that as 2. He explained that that comment related to the whole section that he was surveying not specifically the footpath by the bridge. I found Mr Rowlands to be an honest witness and I accept his evidence about the survey document as truthful. He also gave his opinion about what he saw. He said he saw no obvious defect. I do not rely upon his opinion as to the state of the footpath. He was not familiar with this area. Furthermore, he is not a highways inspector but is a land services officer in the parks department, and has limited training in inspection. Whilst I accept that he genuinely did not consider there were any obvious defects in the footpath calling for any remediable work, his opinion on whether there was a defect did not assist me in reaching my conclusion.*

46. *Mr Misbah is a highway claims officer employed by the defendant and had previously been a highways officer. I did not find his evidence of assistance and he was an unsatisfactory and unreliable witness. He had not visited the site and his views were based on the photographs taken at the time although he admitted that it was not possible to gauge measurements from photographs alone. Furthermore, he was insistent that the footpath was the responsibility of the parks department not the highways department but displayed no understanding of how or why this footpath was in fact a highway maintainable at public expense.*

Ms Mullane also gave evidence. Ms Mullane was the police officer who was responsible for the investigation into the incident. She had in fact been a community policer officer in the 1980s and early 1990s in Llanishen and had used the footpath and the bridge many times. She had never complained about the state of the footpath or the bridge. She expressed her view, however, that when she visited the site again in about December 2011 she thought the area was dark and dangerous. Her view was based on the fact that the footbridge had been designed in a way in which in her view the railings were not long enough and there was a significant drop on either side of the footpath. Ms Mullane is not, however, an expert in engineering or highways and had no background in engineering. She expressed her view as a person visiting the scene. Furthermore, her view was based on the area not on any observed defect in the footpath itself.

As I find that there was no breach of duty, it is not necessary to consider the defence under section 58 of the 1980 Act. I would note that the defendant does not identify the facts on which it relies in its defence. Its evidence on this issue was unclear and inchoate. The defendant's witnesses did not explain clearly why this footpath was left to the responsibility of the parks department and not inspected by the highways department in accordance with any relevant policy on inspections of footpaths even though the defendant accepted that it was a highway maintainable at public expense. ***The defendant did not provide clear evidence as to what policy would have applied if it had been treated as a highway although a document was produced which referred to inspections of adopted footpaths being carried out on a reactive basis, that is in response to a complaint. No witness from the defendant in fact identified that document as containing the current, applicable policy to inspections of footpaths.*** *If I had found that there was an actionable defect which had caused the injury, I would not have found on the evidence before me that the defendant had established the defence in section 58 of the 1980 Act. I would not have been able on the evidence adduced by the defendant to find that it had taken such care as in all the circumstances (including those referred to in section 58(2)) was reasonably required to secure that the relevant part of the highway was not dan-*

gerous. In particular, if there had been a defect, I am not able to tell whether the defendant knew, or could have been expected to know, the condition of the highway given the absence of evidence about the applicable inspection regime for this footpath and, indeed, the evidence, that the footpath was not inspected by the highways department of the defendant and was only considered as part of the parks services.

Key Points

1. The question in each case is whether the particular spot where the claimant tripped or fell was dangerous. If it was, then the defendant authority concedes that there was a failure to maintain the highway and the claimant would be entitled to recover. But if the particular spot was not dangerous, then it is irrelevant that there were other spots nearby that were dangerous or that the area as a whole was due for resurfacing.

2. When a claimant in a trip case claims that she fell by reason of the dangerous condition of the pavement, she must indicate where and how she fell and she must prove it; and it is then for the court to consider whether the place where she fell constituted a danger for which the local authority could properly be held liable.

3. Thus the test of dangerousness is one of reasonable foresight of harm to users of the highway. But in drawing the inference of dangerousness the court must not set too high a standard. Any defect, if its uncorrected presence is to impose a liability, must therefore be such that failure to repair shows a breach of duty.

Occupiers Act 1957 – Edwards v Sutton [2016] EWCA Civ 1005

An ornamental bridge in a local authority park which crossed a stream with rocks in and had a low parapet presented, objectively, a danger from "the state of the premises" within the Occupiers' Liability Act 1957 s.1 such as to give rise to a common law duty of care. However, the danger was obvious to users, and occupiers were not duty-bound to protect against obvious dangers. A formal risk assessment would not have lessened the accident risk, and the provision of side barriers would not have been proportionate. The Judgment said:-

> *"Discussion and my conclusions*
>
> *The claim was brought under the Occupiers' Liability Act 1957.*
>
> *The relevant provisions are sections 1(1) and 2(1), (2) and (3) the Act. They provide as follows:*
>
>> *"1. Preliminary*
>>
>> *(1) The rules enacted by the two next following sections shall have effect, in place of the rules of the common law, to regulate the duty which an occupier of premises owes to his visitors in respect of dangers due to the state of the premises or to things done or omitted to be done on them...."*
>>
>> *"2. Extent of occupier's ordinary duty*
>>
>> *(1) An occupier of premises owes the same duty, the "common duty of care", to all his visitors, except in so far as he is free to and does extend, restrict, modify or exclude his duty to any visitor or visitors by agreement or otherwise.*
>>
>> *(2) The common duty of care is a duty to take such care as in all the circumstances of the case is reasonable to see that the visitor will be reasonably safe in using the premises for the purposes for which he is invited or permitted by the occupier to be there.*
>>
>> *(3) The circumstances relevant for the present purpose include the degree of care, and of want of care, which would ordinarily*

> *be looked for in such a visitor, so that (for example) in proper cases—*
>
> *(a) an occupier must be prepared for children to be less careful than adults; and*
>
> *(b) an occupier may expect that a person, in the exercise of his calling, will appreciate and guard against any special risks ordinarily incident to it, so far as the occupier leaves him free to do so....*"

The judge perceived there to be a contrast between those provisions and the parallel provisions of the Occupiers' Liability Act 1984 regulating the duties owed to persons other than visitors, i.e. principally trespassers. As noted above, the judge said (in the passage quoted above) that section 2 of the 1957 Act did not demand the safety of the premises as such but that the visitor be "safe in using the premises for the purpose for which he or she is invited or permitted by the occupier to be there". He contrasted this with the words of section 1(1) of the 1984 Act which provides as follows:

> *"(1) The rules enacted by this section shall have effect, in place of the rules of the common law, to determine-*
>
> *(a) whether any duty is owed by a person as occupier of premises to persons other than his visitors in respect of any risk of their suffering injury on the premises by reason of any danger due to the state of the premises or to things done or omitted to be done on them; and*
>
> *(b) if so, what that duty is."*

36. *It seems to me, however, that the terms of section 1 of the 1957 Act and section 1(1) of the 1984 Act are not materially different in the relevant respects. Both Acts regulate the different duties imposed on an occupier, in respect of visitors and others, "[in respect of*

dangers/by reason of any danger] due to the state of the premises or things done or omitted to be done on them".

37. *Thus, as it seems to me, it is necessary to identify what danger(s) there is/are before one can see to what (if anything) the occupier's duty in each case attaches. That that approach is necessary is clear from the speech of Lord Hobhouse in Tomlinson's case at paragraphs 69 to 70 and the speech of Lord Hoffmann at paragraph 29. For my part, I do not think that the judge focused adequately on this issue. The case cited by the judge in paragraph 46 of the judgment: Hughes v Lord Advocate, was one in which there was a clear potential danger presented by the lighted lamp. It was, as Lord Reid put it, "a known source of danger" ([1963] AC at p.845).*

38. *Mr McDermott argued at our hearing that the danger presented in this case was "simple" and the judge did not have to be precise. However, when pressed further on the point by the court, he said that danger "due to the state of the premises" was the low parapets and the potential for a fall on to rocks. As for "things done" on the premises, Mr McDermott pointed to the actions of persons such as the claimant wheeling a bicycle as they are permitted to do. With regard to "things...omitted to be done" he relied upon the failure to provide guard rails.*

40. *Looking first at "things done or omitted to be done", I find it hard to see how this activity on Mr Edwards' own part, of walking with his bicycle over this bridge, constituted a danger for these purposes and the failure to provide guard rails seems to me to add nothing at all to whatever may be derived as a danger arising from the "state of the premises".*

41. *Looking then at "the state of the premises", i.e. of the bridge, it is impossible to see how the third and fourth features identified by the judge in paragraph 43 of the judgment could be material: there was no suggestion that the "tarmac fillet", placed to rectify a tripping hazard, or the join between the bridge's surface and the pathway played any part in Mr Edwards' accident. That leaves, in effect, the*

acknowledgment by Mr Scandachanmugasran that the low parapet could be dangerous as the only feature of "danger" from the physical state of the bridge. In this regard, the expert witness, Mr Alford, said that the sides of the bridge were "effectively unguarded". Therefore, he saw no difference between a bridge with low parapets and a bridge with no side barriers at all, while the judge seems to have seen some additional peril from the potential for a pivot over a parapet, adding to the danger of a fall. Of course, whether the danger is such as to trigger the duty under the Act is a matter of evaluation for the court nonetheless.

42. *One can see that an unfenced bridge or a bridge with low parapets will present more danger of a fall than would a bridge with high guard rails. There are, of course, many such unprotected bridges up and down the country in all sorts of locations. In argument, we discussed golf courses, where plank bridges, with no side rails, crossing over ditches are common and have to be negotiated by golfers with trolleys. Ornamental bridges with low walls, together with water features, are likely to be common features of decoration in public gardens. Any structure of this type presents the risk that the user may fall from it. Unlike natural land features, such as steep slopes or difficult terrain or cliffs close to coastal paths, which Lord Hobhouse in Tomlinson said could hardly be described as part of the "state of the premises", it seems to me that a bridge with no sides or only low ones may present a danger from the "state of the premises" such as to give rise to the common duty of care. However, while I am prepared to assume that there was objectively a "danger" arising from the state of the premises in this respect here, does this mean that, in order to discharge the common duty of care, arising from that objective possibility of danger, no such bridges must be left open to visitors or must not be left open to visitors without guard rails or express warnings? In my judgment, the answer to this question is a clear "no".*

43. *The reason for this answer lies, I think, in two well recognised principles of law. First, there is the proper treatment in law of the concept of risk. Secondly, occupiers of land are not under a duty to*

protect, or even to warn, against obvious dangers. Both these propositions appear in the speeches in Tomlinson's case.

44. *The first proposition can be taken from the speech of Lord Hobhouse at paragraphs 79 and 80 as follows:*

> *"79. To suffer a broken neck and paralysis for life could hardly be a more serious injury; any loss of life is a consequence of the greatest seriousness. There was undoubtedly a risk of drowning for inexperienced, incompetent or drunken swimmers in the deeper parts of the mere or in patches of weed when they were out of their depth although no lives had actually been lost. But there was no evidence of any incident where anyone before the claimant had broken his neck by plunging from a standing position and striking his head on the smooth sandy bottom on which he was standing... The park had been open to the public since about 1982. Some 160,000 people used to visit the park in a year. Up to 200 would be bathing in the mere on a fine summer's day. Yet the number of incidents involving the mere were so few. It is a fallacy to say that because drowning is a serious matter there is therefore a serious risk of drowning. In truth the risk of a drowning was very low indeed and there had never actually been one and the accident suffered by the claimant was unique. Whilst broken necks can result from incautious or reckless diving, the probability of one being suffered in the circumstances of the claimant were so remote that the risk was minimal. The internal reports before his accident make the common but elementary error of confusing the seriousness of the outcome with the degree of risk that it will occur.*
>
> *80. The third point is that this confusion leads to the erroneous conclusion that there was a significant risk of injury presented to the claimant when he went into the shallow water on the day in question. One cannot say that there was no risk of injury because we know now what happened. But, in my view, it was objectively so small a risk as not to trigger section 1(1) of the 1984 Act, otherwise every injury would suffice because it*

must imply the existence of some risk. However, and probably more importantly, the degree of risk is central to the assessment of what reasonably should be expected of the occupier and what would be a reasonable response to the existence of that degree of risk. The response should be appropriate and proportionate to both the degree of risk and the seriousness of the outcome at risk. If the risk of serious injury is so slight and remote that it is highly unlikely ever to materialise, it may well be that it is not reasonable to expect the occupier to take any steps to protect anyone against it. The law does not require disproportionate or unreasonable responses."

45. ***A similar statement appears in the speech of Lord Oaksey in Bolton v Stone [1951] AC 850, 863 as follows:***

"The standard of care in the law of negligence is the standard of an ordinary careful man, but in my opinion an ordinary careful man does not take precautions against every foreseeable risk. He can, of course, foresee the possibility of many risks, but life would be almost impossible if he were to attempt to take precautions against every risk which he can foresee. He takes precautions against risks which are reasonably likely to happen. Many foreseeable risks are extremely unlikely to happen and cannot be guarded against, except by the most complete isolation."

Allied with the issue of foreseeability of likelihood risk is the balance of risk, gravity of injury, cost and social value. As to this, I would refer to paragraph 34 of Lord Hoffmann's speech in Tomlinson:

"The balance of risk, gravity of injury, cost and social value

34. My Lords, the majority of the Court of Appeal appear to have proceeded on the basis that if there was a foreseeable risk of serious injury, the council was under a duty to do what was necessary to prevent it. But this in my opinion is an over- simplification. Even in the case of the duty owed to

a lawful visitor under section 2(2) of the 1957 Act and even if the risk had been attributable to the state of the premises rather than the acts of Mr Tomlinson, the question of what amounts to "such care as in all the circumstances of the case is reasonable" depends upon assessing, as in the case of common law negligence, not only the likelihood that someone may be injured and the seriousness of the injury which may occur, but also the social value of the activity which gives rise to the risk and the cost of preventative measures. These factors have to be balanced against each other." While there are limits on social value in a case of this sort, the amenity of this bridge as a feature in the park should not be ignored entirely.

The second proposition is, in my judgment, a particularly forceful consideration in this case. That there was some risk of a fall and the potential for injury must have been obvious. The approach to the bridge was clear and unobstructed. The width of the bridge and the height of the parapets were also obvious to the eye. The bridge was also over water, with whatever might lie beneath its surface. Any user of the bridge would appreciate the need to take care and any user limiting the width of the bridge's track, by pushing a bicycle to his side, would see the need to take extra care.

In my judgment, the present case is similar to Staples v W. Dorset DC [1995] PIQR 439. In that case, the defendant council was the "occupier" of the Cobb, a harbour wall at Lyme Regis to which the public had access as a promenade. The wall sloped downwards towards the sea. The surface had a tendency to slipperiness when wet. It had a drop of 20 feet to rocks on one side and one of 8 feet to a lower walkway on the other. The plaintiff, positioned some 3 feet from the edge, crouched to take a photograph, lost his footing and fell from the wall sustaining injury. There were no warning signs against a slippery surface. The judge held

that there should have been. That decision was reversed on appeal. This court held that a warning would not have told the plaintiff anything that he did not know from his own observation; the most that could be said was that if there had been a notice the plaintiff might have behaved with more circumspection, but a bare possibility was not enough to establish causation in any event.

It was common ground that the duty of care under the 1957 Act arose in that case. However, there was no liability for failure to warn. Kennedy LJ said:

> *"It is, in my judgment, of significance that the duty is a duty owed by the occupier to the individual visitor, so that it can only be said that there was a duty to warn if without a warning the visitor in question would have been unaware of the nature and extent of the risk. As the statute makes clear, there may be circumstances in which even an explicit warning will not absolve the occupier from liability (see s.4(a) above); but if the danger is obvious, the visitor is able to appreciate it, he is not under any kind of pressure and he is free to do what is necessary for his own safety, then no warning is required. So, for example, it is unnecessary to warn an adult of sound mind that it is dangerous to go near the edge of an obvious cliff (see Cotton v. Derbyshire Dales District Council (June 10, 1994, C.A., unreported). In the present case, as Mr Tyson for the respondent acknowledges, he must succeed under the Occupiers' Liability Act or fail, because, although the judge also referred to negligence at common law, there was no other relationship between these parties that could give rise to liability."*

Evans LJ added this:

> *"I find myself driven to the conclusion that the respondent cannot attribute negligence to the appellants in circumstances where nothing was known to them, or would have been known to them if previous inspections had been made, which he did not know and appreciate for himself. If the cause of his accident was the general state of the algae-covered strip at the seaward edge of the Cobb, combined with the pronounced 1:5 slope of the top, then the danger posed was obvious and in fact was appreciated by him. If the cause was an isolated slippery path, which had not manifested itself as a source of potential danger during the 165-year history of the Cobb, then that was not something which the appellants should have foreseen, nor is it clear what the terms of a specific warning would have been. Whichever it was, the appellants cannot be held liable in negligence by reason of their failure to erect warning notices before his accident occurred."*

Nourse LJ agreed with both judgments.

49. *The court also found that it was in as good a position to evaluate the question of liability as had been the trial judge; nothing turned on an assessment of witnesses. To my mind, the same is true here, having proper regard to the principles emerging from Re B (supra).*

51. *A notable feature of the Staples case was the absence of previous accidents, which was perhaps surprising given the nature of the structure, its location and its tendency to be slippery. The absence of accidents is an important feature in the case before us. There is no recorded accident of any character, let alone with the type of consequence that befell Mr Edwards. When weighing up the remarks of Lord Oaksey and of Lord Hobhouse (quoted above) in the context of this case, it appears to me that the probability of such an accident could properly have been sufficiently remote that the risk could be regarded as minimal.*

52. *That brings me to certain additional features of the case with which I should deal: a) the photograph, presented as potential fresh*

evidence; b) risk assessments (or their absence); c) the need (if any) to bring the bridge up to "modern" standards of protection for users.

53. *On the first point, the photograph, I have considered its features very carefully. Out of a sense of overall justice to a severely injured claimant, we should, I believe, admit it formally into evidence. It is designed to show, as already mentioned, that the metalled footway leading to the bridge may not have been present in 1987, when the photograph was taken, and thus that the users of the bridge in earlier years may have been fewer than in more recent times. Accordingly, it is argued, the potential for accidents to have occurred may have been considerably less than contended for by Sutton.*

54. *The photograph has its limitations. It is an aerial image taken from a significant height. The bridge itself and its immediate access is obscured by a tree. It does not show that access to the bridge was barred and we cannot know what facility for access there was. Equally, there is no doubt that there has been a path to the bridge for some time and no evidence suggested that it was a merely recent addition at the time of Mr Edwards' accident. Therefore, Sutton is entitled to say that the absence of recorded accidents is significant. I do not consider that the admission of the photograph into evidence alters the balance of argument to any significant extent for or against either party.*

55. *The judge took the view that the risk posed by the bridge should have been formally identified and assessed. He was influenced by the decision of this court in Uren v Corporate Leisure (UK) Ltd. and in particular the remarks of Smith LJ which I have quoted above. Mr Warnock pointed out all the cases (bar one) cited by Mr McDermott are decisions made in an employment law context where the employer's duty is to take positive thought for the safety of employees beyond that owed to the general public. The one exception was Corbett v Cumbria Kart Racing Club [2013] EWHC 1362 (QB) (King J), which involved the conduct of a hazardous activity, namely a karting race in which it could well be envisaged that there were*

risks to the safety of spectators and assessment of potential risk to them was obviously important.

56. *Mr Warnock also submits that the court must ask what a formal risk assessment would have produced in this case. He relied upon comments of Floyd LJ in Nicholls v Ladbrokes Betting & Gaming Ltd. [2013] EWCA Civ 1963 where it is pointed out that without a finding of what a risk assessment would have produced, the absence of such an assessment does not help a claimant.*

57. ***On the facts of this case likewise, I do not see what a formal assessment would have produced (if anything at all) beyond a statement of the obvious, namely that this was a bridge with low parapets over water; persons not exercising proper care might fall off. I do not see how such a statement would have led to steps being taken that would have prevented or lessened the possibility of Mr Edwards' accident occurring.***

58. *In resisting Mr Edwards' cross-appeal against the judge's finding that there was no obligation on Sutton to erect side barriers on the bridge, Mr Warnock relies heavily upon this court's decision in Japp v Virgin Holidays Ltd. [2013] PIQR 8 in which a holiday-maker sued a tour operator in respect of an injury suffered when she walked into a glass sliding door on a hotel balcony. It was argued for her that the glass in the door failed to meet contemporary standards requiring the use of safety glass in this type of building. The court held that in deciding whether a structural feature complies with local standards, the starting point had to be the standards applicable at the date of design and construction. I have quoted above the relevant passage from the judgment of Richards LJ, with whom Tomlinson LJ and my Lord, Lewison LJ agreed,*

59. ***Mr Warnock submits that in this case there were no standards, concerning side- barriers, which were directly applicable to this bridge and that, therefore, there can be no requirement upon Sutton to update the structure so as to accord with the type of***

standard referred to by Mr Alford as being called for on modern bridges.

60. ***I agree that the existence of new standards for side barriers to be fitted to new and different structures cannot necessarily lead to a conclusion that an occupier is liable in negligence if an older structure does not meet those standards. I do not consider, however, that such an argument necessarily relieves an occupier of liability for breach of the common duty of care when an accident, for which a serious risk of occurrence exists, results from a dangerous state of premises which could readily be remedied by proportionate works of renovation. For the purposes of the present case nonetheless, it seems to me that there was no requirement to provide this bridge with the type of side barriers advocated on Mr Edwards' behalf. Such additions would have altered the character of the bridge significantly and to an extent out of proportion to a remote risk which had never materialised in its known history.***

61. *Mr Edwards has suffered injury which can evoke nothing but the most enormous sympathy. However, in line with the authority which I have endeavored to cite, I find myself in agreement with Mr Warnock's final submission in opening Sutton's appeal that not every accident (even if it has serious consequences) has to have been the fault of another; and an occupier is not an insurer against injuries sustained on his premises. In my judgment, like the court in Staples' case, I think that the standard was set too high by the judge below and I would allow this appeal and would dismiss the cross appeal"*

Key Points

1. It is necessary to identify what danger(s) there is/are before one can see to what (if anything) the occupier's duty in each case attaches.

2. Whether the danger is such as to trigger the duty under the Act is a matter of evaluation for the court.

3. The standard of care in the law of negligence is the standard of an ordinary careful man, and an ordinary careful man does not take precautions against every foreseeable risk.

4. If the danger is obvious, the visitor is able to appreciate it, he is not under any kind of pressure and he is free to do what is necessary for his own safety, then no warning is required. So, for example, it is unnecessary to warn an adult of sound mind that it is dangerous to go near the edge of an obvious cliff.

Defective Premises Act 1972

GILLIAN DRYSDALE v JOANNE HEDGES (2012) - A landlord owed no duty of care under the 1972 Act.

The Judgment set out as follows:-

> ***Breach of the duty in contract and/or under Section 4 of the Defective Premises Act 1972***
>
> ***The terms of the tenancy agreement***
>
> ***78. The premises demised was "All those premises known as 3 Canning Street...".***
>
> *79. Clauses 2.1-2.11 made provision for the tenant's responsibility for the interior of the premises, fixtures and fittings, appliances and like matters. Clause 2.11 granted the landlord access on notice to enter the premises to inspect the state of repair and decoration thereof "and to paint the outside of the Premises or Building and generally to carry out therein or therefrom any repairs, additions, alterations or other works which may appear to the Landlady...to be necessary to the Premises or Under the heading "Cleaning" Clauses 2.15 -2.17 dealt with chimneys, the insides of windows and smoke alarms. By Clause*

2.18 the tenant was not to cause or allow obstructions/blockages concerning internal plumbing, drains downpipes and gutters.

By Clause 2.32 the tenant covenanted not to carry out any decoration to the Premises without prior consent and not to "alter nor interfere with the construction or arrangement of the Premises" without consent.

80. The Landlord's covenants were contained in Clause 3 the relevant subclause of which is 3.2 whereby the landlord covenanted:

> *"3.2 To provide and maintain the structure and exterior...in good repair....except in respect of damage caused by the Tenant or any invitee or insofar as the Tenant is liable to keep the Premises in repair under clause 2 of this agreement."*

Section 4 of the Defective Premises Act 1972

81. This provides:

> *"Landlord's duty of care in virtue of obligation or right to repair premises demised.*
>
> ***(1) Where premises are let under a tenancy which puts on the landlord an obligation to the tenant for the maintenance or repair of the premises, the landlord owes to all persons who might reasonably be expected to be affected by defects in the state of the premises a duty to take such care as is reasonable in all the circumstances to see that they are reasonably safe from personal injury or from damage to their property caused by a relevant defect.***
>
> ***(2) The said duty is owed if the landlord knows (whether as the result of being notified by the tenant or otherwise) or if he ought in all the circumstances to have known of the relevant defect.***

(3) In this section "relevant defect" means a defect in the state of the premises existing at or after the material time and arising from, or continuing because of, an act or omission by the landlord which constitutes or would if he had had notice of the defect, have constituted a failure by him to carry out his obligation to the tenant for the maintenance or repair of the premises; and for the purposes of the foregoing provision "the material time" means—

(a) where the tenancy commenced before this Act, the commencement of this Act; and

(b) in all other cases, the earliest of the following times, that is to say—

(i) the time when the tenancy commences;

(ii) the time when the tenancy agreement is entered into;

(iii) the time when possession is taken of the premises in contemplation of the letting.

(4) Where premises are let under a tenancy which expressly or impliedly gives the landlord the right to enter the premises to carry out any description of maintenance or repair of the premises, then, as from the time when he first is, or by notice or otherwise can put himself, in a position to exercise the right and so long as he is or can put himself in that position, he shall be treated for the purposes of subsection (1) to (3) above (but for no other purpose) as if he were under an obligation to the tenant for that description of maintenance or repair of the premises; but the landlord shall not owe the tenant any duty by virtue of this subsection in respect of any defect in the state of the premises arising from, or continuing because of, a failure to carry out an obligation expressly imposed on the tenant by the tenancy.

> ***(5) For the purposes of this section obligations imposed or rights given by any enactment in virtue of a tenancy shall be treated as imposed or given by the tenancy.***
>
> ***(6) This section applies to a right of occupation given by contract or any enactment and not amounting to a tenancy as if the right were a tenancy, and "tenancy" and cognate expressions shall be construed accordingly."***

I have highlighted what I consider to be the relevant parts of the section.

In order to show a breach of Clause 3.2 and/or Section 4 the Claimant has to show the premises were "not in good repair". On the meaning of "repair" Mr Fetto drew my attention to Quick v Taff Ely Borough Council [1986] QB 809 where Lawton LJ at p 821 stated:

> *"that which requires repair is in a condition worse than it was at some earlier time".*

In the same case Dillon LJ cited with approval the earlier words of Atkin LJ in Anstruther-Gough-Calthorpe v Mc Oscar [1924] 1 KB 716 at p 734 that repair "constitutes the idea of making good damage so as to leave the subject so far as possible as though it had not been damaged".

82.In Alker v Collingwood [2007] 1 WLR 2230 the Court of Appeal had to consider whether a landlord was liable under Section 4 of the 1972 Act for injuries caused to a tenant whose arm went through a glass panel in her front door. The panel was made of ordinary not safety glass. Breach of duty at common law had been abandoned below and the court was concerned essentially with whether or not the unstrengthened glass was "a relevant defect" for the purposes of the 1972 Act. The Claimant's case was that there was a relevant defect because it was dangerous. The Defendant's case was that the glass did not require repair.

83.Laws LJ, with whom Carnwath LJ agreed, stated a duty to repair could not be equated with a duty to make safe and that a duty to keep "in good condition" could not encompass a duty to put in a safe condition. He added this at p 2236:

> ***"A house may offer many hazards : a very steep stairway with no railings ; a hidden step ; some other hazard inside or outside the house of the kind often found perhaps in particular older properties. I do not think it can be said that the Act requires a landlord on proof only of the conditions I have described for the application of Section 4 to make safe any such dangerous feature."***

His approach echoes that of Lawton LJ in Quick who said at p821:

> ***"..a tenant must take the house as he finds it; neither a landlord nor a tenant is bound to provide the other with a better house than there was to start with".***

84.As regards the unguarded drop Mr Fetto accepts that there is no evidence that the wall at the time of the accident was any different from when the Defendant acquired the property. It cannot be said that it was out of repair.

85.As regards the steps Mr Fetto says this. The stone steps unpainted were in good repair. Painted they became less slip resistant and more prone to become slippery when wet or contaminated. Therefore they required repair. He accepts that context is important but submits that the function of the steps was to provide safe access and that that function was undermined when the steps became slippery because of the paint. He says that the court should bear in mind that those using the steps may be carrying objects of different shapes and sizes, that the steps were not protected against the elements and that they were alongside the unguarded drop.

86. This argument is semantically attractive. However, I consider it is stretching the meaning of the word "repair" to apply it to the removal of the paint. The paint did not replace the stone but was additional to it. The stone did not require repair. The paint did not require repair: what it required was removal.

87. I would therefore not find on the facts of this case that the presence of the paint caused the steps not to be "in good repair". Accordingly the presence of the paint did not give rise to a breach of Clause 3.2 and Section 4 of the 1972 Act.

<u>Key Points</u>

1. In order to show a breach of Section 4 the Claimant has to show the premises were "not in good repair"

2. Quick v Taff Ely Borough Council [1986] QB 809 where Lawton LJ at p 821 stated : "that which requires repair is in a condition worse than it was at some earlier time".

3. A duty to repair could not be equated with a duty to make safe and that a duty to keep "in good condition" could not encompass a duty to put in a safe condition.

CHAPTER FOUR
NIHL CLAIMS – UPDATES, CASES AND KEY DECISIONS

The case of Wignall v Secretary of State for Transport (2016), considered a range of issues in NIHL cases as follows:-

> *"The particulars of negligence as pleaded in paragraph 6 of the particulars of claim (page 7) do not all apply to BR.* ***In particular, the provisions of the Factories Act 1961*** *did not apply to the deceased's employment with BR and the references to the statute were directed at the other two Defendants. As against BR, in essence, the deceased alleged that he had been exposed to excessive noise without provision of personal hearing protection, BR having failed properly or at all to commission or carry out any or any adequate noise surveys and having failed to provide him with suitable and sufficient information or instruction or training in respect of the risk that his hearing might be damaged by exposure to noise. He alleged that BR knew or ought to have known that exposure to excessive noise could cause deafness, having regard to the nature of his employment with them.* ***The conventional references to various publications were included, culminating (for the purpose of his claim against BR) in the pleading of the publication by the Ministry of Labour in 1963 of the pamphlet Noise and the Worker****. The deceased recognised that his claim was ostensibly out of time, having regard to the applicable three year limitation period, but he pleaded that his date of knowledge for limitation purposes had not arisen until about 2010, that is to say less than three years before the commencement of the proceedings. By paragraph 8 of its defence (page 16) BR neither admitted nor denied this date of knowledge, but reserved its position on limitation and effectively put him to proof. Indeed the Claimant does bear the burden of proof in relation to establishing that this claim has been brought within the statutory limitation period.*

11. In my judgment, it was implicit, having regard to the dates of employment pleaded, that the deceased was seeking to claim damages for hearing loss attributable to alleged exposure to excessive noise throughout his period of employment commencing in and continuing after 1957. ***In order to succeed in a claim for damages for noise-induced hearing loss, an employee must establish on the balance of probabilities not only that he was exposed to excessive noise (according to the recognised criteria applicable at the relevant time) but also that the employer was in breach of its duty to him to take reasonable care for his health, safety and welfare by preventing or minimising such exposure. This latter carries with it the need to prove that the employer had actual or constructive 'guilty' knowledge, that is to say was aware or ought to have been aware of the relevant risk.*** *In order to recover damages, the deceased would have to prove that BR was in breach of duty.* ***However, given that the conventional starting date for awareness by the average employer of the risk of damage to his employee's hearing through noise is taken to be 1963, following the publication of Noise and the Worker, the defence pleaded at paragraph 4.5 (page 15) that the earliest date on which liability could arise in this claim was 1963 in accordance with that convention.*** *This pleaded defence was without prejudice to the averment that, although it was admitted that a fireman on steam locomotives would not have been provided with hearing protection during the period of the deceased's employment, nevertheless there was no breach of duty because work on steam locomotives was "not known to be excessively noisy and such measures were not necessary" and in any event that the "use of hearing protection on the footplate would have been unsafe": see paragraph 4.4 of the defence (page 14)"*

The Court in *Wignall* gave detailed consideration to the common law duty of care in NIHL cases and said as follows:-

DUTY OF CARE

At common law, an employer owes a duty to take reasonable care for the health, safety and welfare of its employees. This duty is owed to each employee as an individual. The well-known formulation of the duty by Swanwick J. in ***Stokes v Guest, Keen and Nettlefold (Bolts and Nuts) Ltd [1968] 1 WLR 1776 at p.1783*** *is a useful starting point:–*

> *"... The overall test is still the conduct of the reasonable and prudent employer, taking positive thought for the safety of his workers in light of what he knows or ought to know. Where there is a recognised general practice which has been followed for a substantial period in similar circumstances without mishap, he is entitled to follow it unless, in the light of commonsense or newer knowledge, it is clearly bad. But where there is developing knowledge, he must keep reasonably abreast of it and not be too slow to apply it. Where he has, in fact, a greater than average knowledge of the risk, he may therefore be obliged to take more than average or standard precautions. He must weigh up the risk in terms of the likelihood of injury occurring and the potential consequences if it does; and he must balance against this the probable effectiveness of the precautions that can be taken to meet it and the expense and inconvenience they involve. If he is found to have fallen below the standard to be properly expected of a reasonable and prudent employer in these respects, he is negligent." (Emphasis mine).*

In this case, the question arises as to the date from which BR was on notice of the risk of damage to the hearing of employees and in particular those working on and around working steam locomotives, through noise. By reference to ***Thompson v Smiths Shiprepairers (North Shields) Ltd [1984] QB 405****, BR would, as in the case of any large but average employer then in business, have had actual knowledge of this risk with effect from 1963 when they would have become aware of "Noise and the Worker". This much is, in my judgment, effectively conceded by paragraph 4.5 of the defence (page 8). In the* ***Thompson*** *case at* ***p.423****, Mustill J. formulated a liability test by reference to date of knowledge in these terms:–*

> ***"From what date would a reasonable employer, with proper but not extraordinary solicitude for the welfare of his workers, have identified the problem of excessive noise ..., recognised that it was capable of solution, found the possible solution, weighed up the potential advantages and disadvantages of that solution, decided to adopt it, acquired a supply of the protectors, set in train the programme of education necessary to persuade the men and their representatives that the system was useful and not potentially deleterious, experimented with the system and finally put it into effect?" (Emphasis mine).***

It is interesting to note that Mustill J. referred to the employees' representatives, anticipating by implication that any relevant trade union would have to be consulted and that that union might not, for whatever reasons of its own, be immediately supportive of any change in the system of work. Such was, on the documents presented to me, albeit limited, apparently the position of the main rail union (of which, it is a reasonable inference to infer, in a closed-shop industry at that time, the deceased was probably a member), namely ASLEF.

34. *In* ***Doherty v Rugby Joinery (UK) Limited [2004] ICR 1272 (CA) at [57]****, Auld L.J. said:–*

> *"Whilst the notion of a general 'date of knowledge' may provide a useful starting point for considering the date of knowledge in any particular case, that is all it is. Looking – as a court must – at each case on its own facts,* ***the relevant 'date of knowledge' will vary according, not only to the general nature of the industry in its widest sense ... but also to the particular type of work within the industry that is under consideration, the tools used by the Claimant, the nature and pattern of his use of them and the extent to which ... the employer in those circumstances should have been put on notice that harm might ensue to the Claimant if he, the employer, did not do something about it."***

35. *In terms of noise-induced hearing loss, the accepted position is that for exposures at or above 90 dB(A) Lep,d (terminology used, as I understand it, to indicate or describe average exposure over notional eight hour working days or shifts) in the absence of greater than average knowledge, liability at common law in industry generally will run from 1963, the date when Noise and the Worker was first published and for exposures at or above 85 dB(A) Lep,d and below 90 dB(A) Lep,d, in the absence of above average knowledge, liability will only run from 1990: see* ***Baker v Quantum Clothing Group [2011] UKSC 17.***

36. *In this case, the Claimant seeks to prove that he was regularly exposed to a level of noise at or above 90 dB(A) during the course of his employment with BR. If, subject to proof that he did suffer noise-induced hearing loss and that it was attributable at least in part to his work with BR, if he is to recover any damages for exposure before 1963 he must prove that BR had "above average knowledge" at an earlier date. In order to do so, as I understood Mr Rigby's submissions, he relies firstly on the decision of Popplewell J. in* ***Kellett v British Rail Engineering Limited (QBD, unreported, 3rd May 1984)*** *in support of the proposition that BR had "guilty knowledge" as far back as 1956 or alternatively, on the correspondence disclosed by the Defendant, in support of the proposition that BR had such knowledge at some later point in time but before 1963.*

37. *This point as to "date of guilty knowledge" was argued before Miss Recorder Ashworth in* ***Tibbs v BRB (Residuary) Limited (Burnley County Court, claim number 1IR25884, unreported, 4th July 2014)*** *and before Mr Recorder Tilbury in* ***Moss v Secretary of State for Transport (Worcester County Court, claim number 0IR00419, unreported, 8th September 2015).*** *It does not appear that the decision in* ***Tibbs*** *was cited to the recorder in the later case of* ***Moss.*** *Indeed* ***Tibbs*** *was only cited before me because the Claimant's medical expert, Mr Zeitoun, had been a witness in that case and mentioned it to the claimant's solicitors in response to the apparent suggestion that this would be the first case of its kind to come to trial, the Claimant's solicitors and counsel having apparently been previ-*

ously unaware of them. It will be noted that the defendants were the same in those trials as the Defendant in the present case although I am not sure that the defence solicitors were the same in both of them. It would appear from both judgments that the two recorders had essentially the same documentation before them as each other and essentially the same documentation as I have before me. The ***Kellett*** *case was relied upon by the claimants in both those cases. In* ***Tibbs*** *the recorder found as a fact that in October 1961 BR had appreciated that men who were working on the locomotives were exposed to levels of noise which potentially could cause damage to hearing and held that BR knew or should have known at that point that there was a risk of injury. Mr Tibbs had been employed as a footplate fireman on steam locomotives but in his case only between 1961 and 1964.*

38. *Interestingly, in that case it had been conceded that Mr Tibbs had been exposed during the course of his employment with BR to levels of noise in excess of 90 dB(A), but there was a joint statement by engineers on both sides (Mr Hill and Mr Worthington) who had apparently reached that agreement. Mr Jackson was not an expert witness in that case. No such concession is made in the present case before me. The decision of Miss Recorder Ashworth in* ***Tibbs*** *was, so far as I am aware, not appealed. However, in* ***Moss****, Mr Recorder Tilbury, having noted that, as in the present case, the defendant admitted that it possessed sufficient knowledge of the risk of damage to the human ear caused by exposure to high levels of noise to render it subject to a relevant duty from 1963 and that, much as in the present case, the claimant asserted that BR had the requisite knowledge from 1955 relying on* ***Kellett****, found that he was prepared to accept that BR had knowledge at an earlier date than 1963, but not before "the diesel reports were obtained in 1962" (see paragraph 58 of his judgment). It may be that Mr Recorder Tilbury saw other or different documents to those before me, because the disclosed documents before me indicate that there were diesel reports in 1961 and steam reports in 1962. Mr Jackson was the single joint engineering expert in* ***Moss*** *and in paragraph 53(6) of his judgment the recorder noted that Mr Jackson had seen documents relating to problems with*

diesel locomotives dating from 1961 but that these had not been produced before him. At all events, the recorder held that ***Kellett*** *was a case dealing with "boilermaker's deafness", that is to say affecting employees working in the engineering workshops, whereas Mr Moss complained of noise exposure whilst working as a fireman between 1956 and 1964. The recorder appears to have held (see paragraph 61 of his judgment) that Mr Moss had not satisfied him that BR had "actual knowledge" before 1963.*

39. *In my judgment the decision of Popplewell J. in* ***Kellett*** *is not directly applicable to the present case. Mr Kellett had worked in the engineering workshops at Crewe, Cheshire, as a fitter from 1955 to 1966. The judge was aware of the decision in* ***Thompson*** *and said (see page 3H of his judgment) that if " ... the plaintiff's case depended solely on the published literature produced I would have been inclined to adopt the view of Mr Justice Mustill ... that 1963 was about the date when the defendant should be found liable and for the same reasons." However, documentary disclosure in that case showed, in his judgment, that the particular defendant, BRE Limited, had the means of knowledge from about 1951 and actual knowledge from 1955. In the present case, the Claimant relies upon the documents referred to in the judgment in* ***Kellett****, which are in the public domain having regard to that judgment, given in public albeit unreported, although no such documents were disclosed in the present case because they appear no longer to exist. Mr Rigby pointed out that correspondence relating to BRE Limited's workshops included letters from "the Chief Medical Officer of British Rail" and from "the Railway Executive" and argued that the knowledge gained in relation to the workshop should have been applied to the locomotives, that is to say not just to the manufacture and repair of the locomotives but to their actual use on the rails. Popplewell J. found that BRE Limited had actual knowledge which was demonstrated by a series of documents starting in November 1955, including documents in which there was reference to the "British Rail Transport Commission" although in fact I believe that the strictly correct title of that public body was simply the "British Transport Commission". In any event, nowhere in the documents to which Popplewell J. made ref-*

> *erence and upon which he relied in support of his finding of actual knowledge, turning the 'innocent' period into the 'guilty' period in 1955, is there any reference to noise exposure generated by the running in service of BR's steam locomotives. It is a remarkable fact that no claim appears to have been made or, if made, succeeded, prior to the three recent claims of which I am aware which were issued nearly 30 years after the* ***Kellett*** *judgment.*
>
> 40. *Essentially, I take the view that* ***Kellett*** *is a decision on its own facts relating to noise exposure of those working within engineering workshops at BRE Limited and to that particular employer's knowledge of the risks in that case. I am prepared to infer that the risks to that type of employee may have been or even were known in general terms to BR as the state monopoly responsible for the running of the railways at that time, but that does not justify the proposition that BR should have investigated the position with regard to another "particular type of work within the industry", that is to say the work of its footplate firemen employees or "the tools used by" those employees, that is to say steam locomotives, to adopt the wording of Auld L.J. in* ***Doherty****. Accordingly, I do not accept that BR's "date of knowledge" in relation to the risks of knowledge of exposure to firemen working on steam locomotives in general passenger and goods service was as early as 1955".*

The 2000 Diagnosis Guidelines were also referenced in the same case, and HHJ Butler said:-

> 56. *Mr Zeitoun accepts the efficacy of what are commonly called the 'Coles, Lutman and Buffin' guidelines (page 281). The guidelines are conventionally named after their authors but are more properly* ***"Guidelines on the diagnosis of noise-induced hearing loss for medicolegal purposes" published in 2000 in the Journal of Clinical Laryngology, (2000) Clin. Otolaryngol. 25, 264-273. I will simply refer to them as "the guidelines".***
>
> 60. *Mr Zeitoun's evidence before me was to the effect that he had applied those guidelines in an orthodox manner, albeit taking into*

account certain atypical features of the audiogram taken for his purposes in **October 2012.** ***On the other hand, to put it mildly, Mr Jones does not "rate" those guidelines. This is demonstrated by the fact that his report contains a three page critique of what he describes as the "Coles, Lutman and Buffin test" (page 238), expressing the opinion that there are "a number of problems" with that test which in his opinion has been "shown to over diagnose noise-induced hearing loss".*** *He criticises the tables used for age-associated hearing loss by the authors of those guidelines, saying that the same are "inaccurate" (see pages 238–241). In his oral evidence he told me that he did not in fact "dismiss" the guidelines "in their entirety". He recognised that a number of other medico-legal experts in this field do accept those guidelines although he mentioned the names of a number of other experts who, he says, would agree with him. Asked in cross-examination by Mr Rigby whether he had applied the guidelines to the audiogram taken for his purposes in February 2014, he replied by saying that he had not done so, that he did not agree with a lot that was in the guidelines, that many people took the same view but, remarkably, he added that "I am the only one who applies it (the test) properly".*

Mr Zeitoun and Mr Jones also gave evidence before Miss Recorder Ashworth in **Tibbs** *and I note that at paragraph 18 of her judgment she said that the two experts "had very different styles". Her view was that Mr Zeitoun gave his evidence in a more measured way than Mr Jones and, with a certain degree of diplomacy, she said that "Mr Jones could not in any way be accused of being reluctant to express his forthright opinion".* ***She preferred the evidence of Mr Zeitoun in that case although it is fair to say that she considered the difference between them to be more a matter of presentation than quality.*** *I regret to say that I do not feel able to be quite so diplomatic. Before me, Mr Jones gave evidence in a way that can only be described as self-reverential and occasionally arrogant, of which latter characteristic his assertion that he was the only expert who actually applies the guidelines properly (notwithstanding that in large measure he did not agree with them and considered them to have no authority beyond the authors themselves) was the starkest example.*

61. ***Where two experts apply the same general methodology but simply come to a different opinion on the facts of a given case, a judge often faces great difficulty in preferring one to the other.*** *In such cases, albeit rarely, a judge may be forced to decide the case on the balance of proof and, taking the view that it is for a claimant to prove on the balance of probabilities that he did suffer noise-induced hearing loss, to apply the burden of proof where the court is unable to choose between the experts. I do not find myself in that position in this case.* ***Where two experts apply different methods of approach and where indeed one of the experts (a) dismisses significant parts of the guidelines applied by the other expert and (b) alternatively asserts that the other expert has not applied the guidelines in an orthodox fashion, it seems to me that I can and should decide between those experts, express a preference for one or the other and make a finding both as to the nature of the deceased's hearing loss and as to causation accordingly.*** *In doing so, I have had regard to the well-known principles stated by the Court of Appeal in* ***Loveday v Renton [1990] 1 Med LR 117 at 125*** *(per Stuart-Smith L.J.) and* ***Transco PLC v Griggs [2003] EWCA Civ 564 at*** *[24] – [26] (per Hale L.J.)* ***and having done so I unhesitatingly prefer and accept the evidence, opinion and conclusions of Mr Zeitoun.*** *In my judgment he has reasonably applied the guidelines, taking proper account of atypical features and expressing his opinion in what was, after exploration in cross-examination by Mr Stewart and in re-examination by Mr Rigby, a measured, cogent and persuasive manner. In explanation of my preference I will refer to the nature of the technical dispute between the two experts and the application of the guidelines to this case.*

63. *For the purposes of Mr Zeitoun's report a pure tone audiogram was performed for him by an audiologist on 18th October 2012 (page 268). It appears at more than one place in the bundle (e.g. page 207). For the purpose of Mr Jones' report a further pure tone audiogram was taken by an audiologist or technician on 18th February 2014 (page 271).* ***As I understood the evidence of both experts, the appearances of those audiograms are quite similar, both demonstrating a hearing loss at the 2 kHz frequency, partic-***

ularly in the right ear, greater than that at the 3 kHz and 4 kHz frequencies. *It appeared to be agreed that this was an atypical appearance. Mr Zeitoun expressed the opinion that it was something he would expect to see and indeed had seen in perhaps 5 to 15% of cases but Mr Jones expressed the opinion that the audiograms simply did not show evidence of noise-induced hearing loss at all because, as an invariable point of principle on his part, hearing losses most marked at 2 kHz are not evidence of NIHL. His opinion was that even if the guidelines were used they could not be used to apply to such losses because they would result in a false diagnosis, this being "one of many flaws" in those guidelines (page 262). This dispute appears to have been the very same issue argued by the same experts in* ***Tibbs*** *where, as in this case, the claimant's loss at 2 kHz was greater than would have been expected for someone of his age. In that case, as in the present case, Mr Zeitoun pointed to the chapter on noise-induced hearing loss in a recognised textbook, Scott-Brown's Otolaryngology (6th Edition) (page 274), the editor of the relevant chapter apparently being one Dr Alberti. In the present case, the first part of the crucial passage at page 2/11/11 of the textbook (page 278) relied upon by* ***Mr Zeitoun states:–***

> ***"Noise-induced permanent threshold shift usually commences between 3 and 6 kHz, often around 4 kHz, and gradually worsens at that frequency and spreads into neighbouring frequencies. At first it may be asymptomatic but if it spreads into the lower frequencies of 3 and 2 kHz complaints begin."***

Pausing there, Mr Zeitoun's opinion is that it is accordingly recognised that noise-induced hearing loss can affect the 2 kHz frequency. As will be seen, he also points out that the guidelines also refer to involvement at 2 kHz in some cases. If this is correct, then Mr Jones' opinion that a loss (or "excess loss") greatest at 2 kHz rather than 3 kHz is not a feature of noise- induced hearing loss and that the audiograms demonstrate that this deceased did not have such loss, cannot be correct or, at the very least, is seriously overstated. The passage from the textbook continues on pages 2/11/11 to 2/11/12 (pages 278, 280 and 279 of the trial bundle in that order, pages 279 and 280 having plainly been inserted in the wrong order):–

> *"'Typical' audiograms are frequently found in texts but they are typical only of the group to which they apply. The 'typical' audiogram shown in Figure 11.12 is quite different from the audiogram shown in Figure 11.7....... It should be remembered that loss from noise is not the total hearing loss in an otherwise otologically normal person. It is the difference between the normal hearing corrected for presbyacusis" (age-associated hearing loss) "and the observed hearing loss. Individual susceptibility varies enormously and unfortunately there is no good way of predicting this."*

***The guidelines do indeed indicate that the normal or typical presentation is of a measurement of hearing threshold level at 3, 4 or 6 kHz which is at least 10 decibels greater than that at 1 or 2 kHz.** It is in my judgment important to bear in mind that guidelines are just that. They are guidelines not a straightjacket. The express purpose of the guidelines is said (page 281) to be:–*

> *"... to assist in the diagnosis of noise-induced hearing loss (NIHL) in medico-legal settings. The task is to distinguish between possibility and probability, the legal criterion being more probable than not. It is argued that the amount of NIHL needed to qualify for that diagnosis is that which is reliably measurable and identifiable on the audiogram. The three main requirements for the diagnosis of NIHL are defined: R1, high frequency hearing impairment; R2, potentially hazardous amount of noise exposure; R3 identifiable high frequency audiometric notch or bulge." (Emphasis mine)*

It is also correct that the guidelines refer, for the most part, to "uncomplicated cases of NIHL", that is to say "typical" NIHL together with presumed "normal" age-associated hearing loss (AAHL): see paragraph 2.1 of the guidelines (page 282). In my

judgment, this plainly does not mean that the guidelines cannot be applied to complicated cases where the NIHL is atypical or the AAHL is abnormal, merely that the expert using the guidelines should recognise the atypicality or abnormality. No doubt in some cases the atypicality and the degree of abnormality would be such as to prevent an expert using the guidelines but I am satisfied on the balance of probabilities that Mr Zeitoun did not find himself in that position. In my judgment he has interpreted the guidelines as a guide not a rigid rule: see paragraph 3.1 (page 282). It is to be noted that the authors of the guidelines considered that they had "been derived after careful consideration of the data available".

65. *I note with interest that in the* ***Moss*** *case, where the defendant (this same Defendant) had no medical expert, leading counsel for the Secretary of State, Mr Limb QC, actually deployed the guidelines against the claimant's expert in an attempt to demonstrate that he had not applied them properly and in the course of that case leading counsel specifically described the guidelines as being "the definitive report in these cases for diagnosis" (see judgment of Mr Recorder Tilbury at paragraph 50). I find it difficult to understand how the Defendant can, in the very next trial on the same point, seek to persuade the court to accept the evidence of an expert who does not accept the efficacy or accuracy of guidelines, far less their definitive nature, when this same Defendant has previously put them forward before a different court on similar facts as being the definitive basis for diagnosis in such cases.*

66. *In my judgment and experience, categorisation of the guidelines as being the definitive basis for such diagnosis in the medico-legal context (whatever might be the case in clinical practice) is justifiable and correct.* ***Requirement 3 (audiometric configuration) paragraph 7.2 (page 283) states that "evidence for NIHL is also provided on the audiogram by a sufficiently large relative bulge downwards and to the left in the 3 to 6 kHz range", it being noted that a notch or a bulge may suffice. In this case Mr Zeitoun expresses the opinion that there is a bulge in the audiogram (page***

268) at 3 kHz: see paragraph 3.2.4 of his report (page 200)*. To the contrary Mr Jones expresses the opinion, certainly by reference to the later audiogram (page 271) that the bulge is not at 3 kHz but at 2 kHz. In cross-examination Mr Zeitoun appeared to modify his opinion at least to the extent of accepting that the bulge might include 2 kHz. As was said in* **Griggs** *the willingness of an expert to reconsider or modify an opinion may well support his credibility rather than damage it. He did not agree with Mr Jones that excess loss at 2 kHz, greater than that at 3 or 4 kHz, contraindicated NIHL or prevented a diagnosis of NIHL, saying that the audiogram was atypical but still within the methodology of the guidelines. He accepted that if the atypicality had included the 1 kHz frequency he would then not have diagnosed NIHL.*

67. For the sake of completeness I should record that the tabular representation of the appearances of the October 2012 audiogram are set out on pages 269 (right ear) and 270 (left ear) in the bundle. The statistically predicted average for the general population of a man of the deceased's then age (70 years) appears at line c, the deceased's actual hearing levels at line a, the adjusted calculation for the loss attributable to age association at line f and the calculation as to the relevant audiometric bulge at line g. I pause to say that Mr Zeitoun's calculation is made by reference to the guidelines and therefore by the use of tables which Mr Jones does not consider to be accurate. The tabular presentation of the audiogram result shows that there is no loss attributable to noise at 4 or 6 kHz on the right side, that there is a loss (13.6 decibels) at 3 kHz but a greater loss (25.8 decibels) at 2 kHz. In the left ear, the pattern is similar although the difference perhaps less marked, there being a small loss (5.4 decibels) at 4 kHz, a large loss (21.6 decibels) at 3 kHz and an even larger loss (29.8 decibels) at 2 kHz. It is, as both experts say, atypical. However, rejecting as I do Mr Jones' opinion that the guidelines are not accurate, efficacious, definitive or applicable to this case the question still remains whether Mr Zeitoun's opinion that the atypical result at 2 kHz is sufficiently within the scope of the guidelines to enable him properly to diagnose NIHL by reference to that methodology. Mr Jones, using tables different to those in the guidelines (derived he said from the National Study of Hearing published in 1991 but which tables were not included in the bundle) made his own calculation which also showed that the greatest loss was at the 2 kHz frequency (14.8 decibels) although it was pointed out that there was at least one, admittedly small, error in his calculations (the excess loss at 3 kHz in the left ear on the 2014 audiogram having been wrongly recorded by him as "45" rather than "55" (page 231).

68. *I have not overlooked the fact that Mr Jones was able to refer (page 242) to a sentence from a publication with which he does agree, that is to say a position paper of the American College of Occupational Medicine (ACOM, 2002). That paper, summarising "the typical features of NIHL" states eight principal characteristics of occupational NIHL, the sixth of which includes the words, "there is always far more loss at 3, 4 and 6 kHz than at 0.5, 1 and 2 kHz" and "the greatest loss usually occurs at 4 kHz". He also referred (page 243) to a publication called Advances in Noise Research (1998) and in particular Chapter 8 thereof on "The clinical diagnosis of noise-induced hearing loss" written by Dr (now Professor) Luxon, which he said endorsed the American criteria, although I note that it does so in slightly different terms, perhaps because it was quoting the 1989 version of the ACOM criteria (see pages 727 – 728) to the same general effect. Mr Jones seizes on the use of the word "always". That is his own opinion and it is unsurprising that he quotes a position paper with which he agrees and which agrees with him (a circular argument worthy of the criticism to the same effect made of Mr Zeitoun about considering the deceased's atypicality to be within the acceptable range because in previous cases in which he had himself diagnosed NIHL such atypicality had been seen). However, Dr Luxon also accepts that NIHL "can begin in frequencies other than the 3 – 6 kHz region" albeit that "this is rare" and should only be accepted in certain circumstances. By necessary implication there could in such cases be a greater loss at 2 kHz. The evidence of Mr Jones before me was that it could never be diagnosed where there was more loss at 2 kHz in any circumstances so his reliance on this reference seems to be somewhat selective.*

69. ***In any event, if the UK guidelines from 2000 are to be regarded as the "definitive" approach in the medico-legal context in English courts, as in my experience is usually the case and as was this same Defendant's position in Moss, then whatever might be the position in a non-forensic clinical diagnostic context in the USA (or even in England), the word "always" cannot be justified in the medico-legal context because the guidelines support the opinion that sometimes, albeit in a small proportion of cases, there can be more loss at 2 kHz.***

70. ***For all the foregoing reasons, I found the opinion of Mr Zeitoun to be logically consistent and his use of the guidelines and his approach to the audiogram results to accord with the orthodox medico-legal approach.*** *Each case depends on its own facts and the quality of the evidence adduced. In the context of this present case, on the evidence presented to me, I reject Mr Jones' opinion that where the greatest loss is at 2 kHz, NIHL cannot ever properly be* ***diagnosed. I accept the opinion of Mr Zeitoun that although the deceased was atypical and his, NIHL in his case could properly be diagnosed, albeit as a rare or minority cases, subject to proof of hazardous noise exposure has been proved. The position is that, on the facts of this case, such exposure has been found proved.***

71. *On the balance of probabilities, having regard to the main area of dispute between the experts, Mr Jones' residual alternative argument that this deceased's hearing loss could be explained by reference to some idiopathic or genetic cause, currently beyond scientific explanation, does not dissuade me from finding that on the balance of probabilities the hazardous noise exposure in the deceased's employment was causative or materially contributory of part of his noise-induced hearing loss.* ***Accordingly, he is entitled to an award of general damages for pain, suffering and loss of amenity to be assessed initially by reference to the totality of NIHL but then apportioned to reflect the portion that can be attributed to this Defendant's breach of duty***

In summary – breach of duty

a) It is generally taken as the date by which the harmful effects of excessive noise were foreseeable.

b) The 1972 publication said that where noise level was above 90DBA, an employer must take steps to reduce the noise, or if this was not practicable, provide hearing protection.

c) The defendant's date of knowledge is not fixed across all industries and all employers. It may vary from industry to industry.

d) The Supreme Court in Baker v Quantum Clothing Group [2011] UKSC 17 confirmed that prior to 1 January 1990, the average employer owed a common-law duty of care to protect employees where their daily noise dose exceeded the 'negligent threshold' of 90dB(A) over eight hours. Baker v Quantum confirmed that the Factories Act applies to NIHL claims.

e) These 1989 noise Regulations came into force on 1 January 1990. They set a First Action Level of 85 db(A) and a Second Action Level of 90 db(A).Regulation 4 – assessment of noise exposure- The employer must risk assess the noise levels where they are above 85db. This will allow them to identify the employees exposed to noise and to take action.At 90 DB Regulation 7 – reduce noise exposure- Every employer shall reduce employee's exposure to noise to below 90db (other than by providing hearing protection)Regulation 8 – ear protection- An employer shall supply employees with hearing protection if they request it when the noise levels are likely to be above 85db. They must supply the protection when the noise levels reach 90db

f) In addition to the obligations placed on employers by the above 1989 Regulations, there are the requirements of the Personal Protective equipment at Work Regulations 1992, and the Management of Health and Safety at Work Regulations of 1992 and 1999.

g) The 2005 Noise Regulations replace the 1989 Noise Regulations and introduce new requirements for action to be taken by employers. For example, the 2005 Regulations require employers to take action to protect workers at levels of noise 5 decibels lower than in the 1989 Regulations and now require health surveillance (hearing checks) for workers regularly exposed above 85 decibels.

CHAPTER FIVE
DISEASE CLAIMS – UPDATES, CASES AND KEY DECISIONS

VWF/ HAVS update – ADRIAN BOWE v MERSEY REWINDS ENGINEERING LTD & ORS (2018)

Principle – A recorder who found that an employee had suffered occasional and transitory exposure to vibration at work, some of which had exceeded the accepted threshold level, had not been entitled to conclude that the employers had breached their duty of care in failing to monitor their employee's use of vibrating tools or warn him of the potential effects on his health. Such a conclusion would need to be supported by a finding as to frequency, and expert evidence about the effect of intermittent use at such a frequency.

> *It was the claimant's case that each defendant was in breach of its duty to take reasonable care to protect him from sustaining injury during the course of his employment. He alleged that frequent and prolonged use of vibrating tools caused him to suffer from vibration white finger (VWF) and carpal tunnel syndrome. The defendants admitted each owed a duty of care to the claimant as claimed. It was agreed at trial that none of the defendants took any steps at any time to warn, advise or monitor the claimant in respect of the potential effects on his health of working with vibrating tools. Each defendant denied that the claimant was subject to frequent or prolonged exposure to vibrating tools as alleged. Breach of duty was denied. Causation was also in issue. The first and third defendants pleaded a limitation defence.*
>
> *A trial was directed of two issues: limitation and breach of duty. The trial took place over 4 days some months apart - 15 and 16 October 2014 and 16 and 17 February 2015. The recorder gave an extempore judgment on 18 February 2015. He dismissed the limitation defence on the grounds that the claimant's date of knowledge*

(as defined in Section 14 Limitation Act 1980) was within the three years before the issue of proceedings. There is no appeal against that determination.

The recorder also concluded that each defendant was in breach of its duty of care to the claimant because over many years it "transitorily" exposed the claimant to vibration speeds above what is known in the industry as "the threshold level" but took no steps to warn him about the potential effects on health of working with vibrating tools, or to monitor his exposure or otherwise to advise him about working with vibrating tools. It is against the finding of breach that the defendants appeal.

Breach of Duty

There was also before the court the publication HS(G) 88, Hand-Arm Vibration, produced by the Health and Safety Executive in 1994. It was part of a series of documents with the purpose of providing guidance for those who have duties under the Health and Safety at Work etc Act 1974. From the opening chapter under key points and throughout, it is made plain that employers must be aware of and guard against the risk of injury where people regularly work with vibrating tools for prolonged periods. This is explicit at paragraph 21 of the document where the following appears "Programmes of preventive measures and health surveillance are recommended where workers' exposure regularly exceeds an A(8) of 2.8m/s2."

The recorder set out at paragraphs 13 and 14 of the judgment the agreed position as to the risk of injury caused by vibration. He observed that throughout the period that the claimant was employed by the three defendants it was agreed that there was a foreseeable risk of injury to a person exposed to levels of vibration of 1m/s2 [A8]. This is generally described as the threshold level. Below that level there was no foreseeable risk of injury resulting from exposure to vibrating tools and employers owed no duty of care at common law. Above that level there was a duty upon an employer at common law and, later, pursuant to the Control of Vibration at Work Regulations 2005, to take some steps to alert employees to the potential risk of injury by warning, monitoring and advising those using vibrating tools. Above the action level ie 2.8m/s2, active steps such as reduction of exposure by modification of tools, job rotation and the like was required. What was omitted from the agreement, but should be taken as read for it accurately to reflect reality, was that isolated exposure to levels above the threshold or action level does not lead to a foreseeable risk of injury. What is required is regular (or, more accurately, frequent) exposure to those levels.

Expert Evidence

The experts' evidence was agreed and so they were not called. They agreed that if the claimant's account of his usage of vibrating tools was accepted then it was very likely that he had been exposed to "a hand/arm vibration dose exceeding the action level on a regular basis dependent upon the actual duration of his average working day". They also agreed that if the defendants' account (as set out in their employees' witness statements) of his usage of vibrating tools was accepted "then it is highly likely that the claimant was not exposed to significant hand/arm vibration." Mr Taylor was asked to define "significant" in this context. It meant exposure to a hand/arm vibration dose exceeding the threshold level.

On Appeal

Mr Woolfenden's submission, repeated before us by Mr Benson QC, was that 30 minutes exposure to a needle gun once a fortnight equates to 3 minutes per working day. Mr Woolfenden urged the recorder to make a finding that the needle gun was used once a fortnight, at least with the first defendant. To that should be added, Mr Benson reminded us, the exposure to the air chisel at or above the threshold level and the fact that the claimant was exposed to these tools over many years.

There are two problems with the approach in respect of the fortnightly use of the needle gun: first there is no expert evidence to suggest that a single occasion of 30 minutes exposure equates to 3 minutes on 10 occasions. ***Second, and more importantly, the recorder made no finding that the claimant used the needle gun once a fortnight or at any other level of frequency or regularity nor did he make any findings about the frequency of use of the air chisel. Having re-read the whole of the lay evidence I am not surprised by this. At its highest the recorder found "transitory" exposure above the threshold. In the absence of any finding as to frequency and any expert evidence about the effect of intermittent use at such a frequency it was not open to the recorder to move from a finding of transitory exposure even over many years to a conclusion that this constituted a breach of duty by the defendants. To come to that conclusion he would have had first to find that the claimant was using the needle gun and/or the air chisel at or above the threshold level on a regular/frequent basis and it was in that situation that there had been no warning, advice, monitoring etc. He did not do so because he was rightly not satisfied on the evidence that the use of vibrating tools was either regular or frequent. The evidence was all the other way.***

It follows that the recorder's conclusion as to breach of duty cannot stand. allow this appeal.

The Findings at the Trial

At paragraph 29 the recorder found (and clarified the finding at 31) that the claimant used needle guns throughout his employment by each defendant and, until 1999, air chisels (except when employed by the second defendant which did not use air chisels.). It is plain from the context that the recorder considered the use of needle guns (throughout) and air chisels (up to 1999) occasional but it took place over many years. He concluded at paragraph 30 that "to the extent the claimant used the need le gun and the air chisel with all the defendants there was a breach of duty "in that he was transitorily...exposed to levels above the threshold." He concluded, "I appreciate that this is probably not helpful to either party – and we have already discussed the constraints within which I have to deal with these matters caused by the splitting of the trial into two parts and the absence of the experts – but there it is. Therefore, to that limited extent, there was a breach of duty in relation to the exposure and there was, therefore, accordingly, a breach of duty in relation to the requirements either at common law or later pursuant to statute following such a breach of the threshold limit". I am quite satisfied that in saying "there was a breach of duty in relation to the exposure" the recorder meant that from time to time the exposure exceeded or breached the threshold level and accordingly, given the absence of any warnings or other advice or monitoring, breach of duty followed.

COSH update – Cotton v Helphire (6) Neutral Citation Number: [2019] EWHC 508 (QB)

Background

Shaun Cotton, the claimant in the action and to whom I shall refer as 'the appellant', appeals with permission against the Judgment of Mr Recorder Clayton sitting in the Leeds County Court handed down on 1st May 2018 following a hearing on 28th February, 1st, 2nd and 20th March 2018, whereby his claim for damages for personal injury and consequential loss for occupational asthma as a result of exposure to chemicals and cleaning products and to exhaust fumes whilst employed by Helphire Limited ('the respondent') was dismissed. Each party is represented on the appeal by their trial counsel, Mr Charles Feeny for the appellant and Miss Jayne Adams QC for the respondent, and I am grateful to them for their written and oral submissions.

The relevant background may be shortly stated. The appellant was employed by the respondent or its predecessors from February 1999 until 2012 as a car valet, checker and driver. His case was that, in breach of the Control of Substances Hazardous to Health Regulations 2002 ("COSHH") and negligently, he was exposed to substances that were hazardous to health. In consequence, he developed occupational asthma. He worked from two premises, initially in Wakefield and then, from 2006, in Leeds, from which time the respondent used a different valeting company, Autoclenz, though it was the appellant's case that he still performed some valeting services at the new premises. He made no complaint, however, about his exposure to chemicals or fumes whilst working at Wakefield. The respondent's case was it was not in breach of any regulation or duty of care, nor was the appellant exposed to fumes or chemicals that gave rise to any foreseeable risk of injury and his asthma was not caused by exposure to workplace substances.

Trial Findings

Although, as originally pleaded, the claim alleged a number of breaches of duty under Regulations and at common law, at trial the appellant principally pursued his case on the basis of a breach of Regulation 11 of COSHH. The substance of his case was that throughout the material period he presented with an asthmatic cough at work, which should have triggered a health surveillance pursuant to Regulation 11 that, in turn would have led to a medical examination or investigation that revealed he was asthmatic and thereby resulted in the respondents taking a number of measures, including the provision of personal protective equipment, or being taken off valeting duties.

The agreed technical evidence was that, given the small amount of substances used by way of cleaning agents in the valeting process and their intermittent use, any exposure to chemicals and substances within the preparations that were hazardous to health (as, indeed, some were according to the manufacturers' data sheets) was probably well below the Workplace Exposure Limits. The respondent's case was that, in these circumstances, the appellant could only succeed on the basis that it had some sort of knowledge of the susceptibility of the appellant to the development or exacerbation of asthma; there was none and so the Regulation was not triggered or, therefore, breached.

The issue of diesel fumes came to nothing and no significance was or could be attached to it. The Recorder found that there was no evidence to support any finding that they added to any 'irritant-load' in relation to the appellant's condition and there is no criticism of that finding.

Causation Findings

Dr Hind was of the opinion that the appellant did not have work related asthma but had constitutional asthma which was eventually triggered to its chronic state by a severe chest infection in January 2011. He accepted that, by reason of his hyper-active airways, he was susceptible to irritation, which may have been as a result of levels of occupational exposure below approved levels, but he did not agree that his asthmatic condition was caused by chemical irritation at work. He based this conclusion on the evidence as to the levels or concentrations of the cleaning agents, the lack of improvement in symptoms once exposure ceased and, most significantly, the medical contemporary records which contradicted the appellant's assertion that his persistent chest symptoms began in 2005.

The Recorder reviewed the evidence of Dr Howard and Dr Hind and made findings in relation to it, specifically preferring the evidence of Dr Hind to that of Dr Howard where there was a conflict of opinion. He found that the appellant had a persistent but unchanging cough throughout the relevant period and that he suffered from a serious viral upper respiratory tract infection in January 2011 that persisted for several months and now had a heightened sensitivity, and that, taking account of the agreed level of exposure of the appellant to any hazardous substances, there was no basis for a finding that the appellant suffered from work related symptoms prior to January 2011.

The Appeal

The Recorder failed to make sufficient findings and/or failed to appreciate the consequences of appropriate findings on two critical issues in the case; that is

a) that the appellant was suffering from a persistent cough whilst working for the respondents; in effect the agreed factual evidence.

b) The cough was a manifestation of the appellant's underlying asthmatic condition caused by chemical irritation at work; in effect the agreed medical evidence.

The Recorder wrongly synthesised the effect of regulation 11 of CSHH, so as to convert the issue of breach of regulations into one of negligence as opposed to the correct legal approach which would involve analysing the precise terms of the statutory duty on the facts of the case. Had the Recorder taken the correct legal approach, he could only have concluded that there was a breach of regulation 11 in circumstances in which the appellant was displaying a respiratory symptom at work in the face of exposure to chemical irritants.

The Recorder expressed a preference for the medical evidence of Dr Hind as to the appellant's work-related symptoms being those of transitory irritation only, whilst failing to appreciate that this aspect of Dr Hind's evidence, as acknowledged by him, was subject to a factual premise that the appellant had not shown any work-related symptoms prior to December 2010. If, as the Recorder had to find on the evidence, the appellant was suffering work-related symptoms for a period of years prior to December 2010, the premise of his evidence was not sustainable and therefore neither was his evidence on this issue.

The Findings

I am not persuaded by the appellant's grounds of appeal. For the reasons advanced by Miss Adams QC, on the evidence before him, the Recorder was entitled to make the findings that he did in relation to the appellant's condition and working conditions over the relevant period and to prefer the opinion of Dr Hind over Dr Howard for the reasons that he gave. On Dr Hind's evidence the appellant did not contract irritant induced occupational asthma. There was no substantive failure by the Recorder to make findings nor are the bases of his findings unclear. Although the appellant had a cough over the relevant period, it was far from agreed medical evidence that it was a manifestation of the appellant's underlying asthmatic condition or that it was caused by chemical irritation at work, for the reasons that he gave.

In my judgment, on the evidence and in the light of the justifiable findings to which the Recorder made, the claim under Regulation 11 was not made out. There was no basis for a finding of liability, not least given the failure of the appellant to establish causation. Accordingly, the appeal is dismissed.

Section 33 and Limitation – RICHARD FUDGE v (1) HAWKINS & HOLMES LTD (2) FG MINTER LTD (2018)

In this action the Claimant, Richard Fudge, who is 81 years of age, seeks provisional damages against each of the Defendants for alleged asbestos-related injury leading to the development of diffuse pleural thickening and asbestosis. He is said to have a respiratory disability of 30%, 20% of which is attributable to pleural thickening and 10% to asbestosis; the disease is likely to increase by 10% in next 10 years. There is said to be a 3% risk of malignant mesothelioma and a 2% risk of asbestos related lung cancer. Life expectancy is alleged to be reduced by 4 months because of the risk of asbestos related malignant disease and by 3 months due to a risk of respiratory failure and also of chest infection.

He alleges that this sad state of affairs has come about because he was exposed to asbestos while working for the Defendants at various separate times between 1973 and 1978, cutting asbestos insulation boards, sweeping asbestos dust and debris, or working near laggers as they worked with asbestos paste. He alleges that each of the Defendants owed him and were in breach of common law and/or statutory duties to protect him from exposure to asbestos and accordingly that each is liable.

The Defendants each deny liability and plead limitation defences.

On 11 September 2017 Master Thornett ordered that there be a preliminary trial on the issue of limitation. This is my judgment on that preliminary issue. It is common ground that the action was brought after the expiry of the limitation period defined by the Claimant's date of knowledge. The Claimant accepts that he had the knowledge for the purpose of sections 11 and 14 of the Limitation Act 1980 by the summer of 2008. Therefore the three year period would have expired in the summer of 2011. The claim form in these proceedings was issued on 9 February 2017, some five and a half years after the expiry of the primary limitation period. Therefore the sole issue is whether I should exercise my discretion under section 33 of the Limitation Act 1980 to disapply the limitation period which the Claimant accepts otherwise bars him from pursuing this claim against all three Defendants.

CHAPTER SIX
EL CLAIMS – UPDATES, CASES AND KEY DECISIONS

Enterprise Act – JANICE COCKERILL v (1) CXK LTD (2) ARTWISE COMMUNITY PARTNERSHIP (2018)

The Facts

An employee who had been injured at work when she fell down a step had not established that either her employer or the occupier of premises had breached the duty of care owed to her. She had not been looking where her feet were going when she fell and had not seen the step, even though it was in plain sight before her, and marked with hazard tape. Key Points about the Enterprise Act considered.

> *69 Civil liability for breach of health and safety duties*
>
> *"(2) Breach of a duty imposed by a statutory instrument containing (whether alone or with other provision) health and safety regulations shall not be actionable except to the extent that regulations under this section so provide.*
>
> *Employer's duty of care*
>
> *The effect in this case of section 69 of the Enterprise and Regulatory Reform Act 2013 ('the 2013 Act'), which amends the Health and Safety at Work etc Act 1974, was not disputed. The case proceeded on the agreed basis that there was no longer a self-standing cause of action available to the claimant for any breaches of the statutory duties of employers under what have become known as the 'six pack' of health and safety regulations.* ***Her only cause of action against CXK lay in common law negligence – in other words, by establishing that the common law duty of care owed to her by her***

employer had been breached, and that that breach had, foreseeably, caused her accident.

But the essence of the employers' duty at common law, briefly stated, is to take reasonable steps to provide a reasonably safe place of work, and system of work, for their employees, so as to protect them, so far as reasonably practicable, from reasonably foreseeable harm. The caselaw is clear about the importance of context, in understanding what is reasonable, and in giving detailed meaning to that duty, in individual cases.

Care is needed with this analysis. ***In removing the claimant's cause of action for breach of statutory duty, the 2013 Act did not repeal the duties themselves.***

Those duties continue to bind employers in law. So they continue to be relevant to the question of what an employer ought reasonably to do. However by enacting s.69, Parliament evidently intended to make a perceptible change in the legal relationship between employers and employees in this respect. It removed direct actionability by claimants from the enforcement mechanisms to which employers are subject in carrying out those statutory duties. *What I have referred to as this 'rebalancing' intended by s.69 was evidently directed to ensuring that any breach of those duties would be actionable by claimants if, but only if, it also amounted to a breach of a duty of care owed to a particular claimant in any given circumstances; or in other words, if the breach was itself negligent.* ***It is no longer enough to demonstrate a breach of the regulations. Not all breaches of the statutory regime will be negligent. Before the 2013 Act, the statutory regime had produced results in which employers were fixed with legal liability for accidents even where they had taken reasonable precautions against them.***

Manual Handling Update – RHONDA STEWART (AKA RHONDA WHITE) v LEWISHAM & GREENWICH NHS TRUST (2017)

The claim was brought in respect of a back injury suffered by the Claimant when lifting an item of work equipment in the course of her employment with the Defendant as a Community Midwife.

She alleged breach by the Defendant of the Management of Health and Safety at Work Regulations 1999, of the Manual Handling Regulations 1992 and of its common law duty of care.

The Court held a judge had correctly held that the failure to carry out a risk assessment regarding the lifting of a box did not breach the Manual Handling Operations Regulations 1992, in circumstances where the claimant had not shown that there had been a real risk of injury.

At [38] the Recorder stated:

> *"It is for the Claimant to satisfy me on the balance of probabilities that a risk assessment of a type not carried out was required and I am not satisfied as to that here."*

The Claimant submits that the Recorder misdirected himself when holding that the Claimant bore the burden of showing that a risk assessment was required and ought instead to have found that the Defendant bore, and had failed to discharge, the burden of showing that an assessment was not required.

23. It is submitted that this was a case in which there was a real risk of injury as borne out by the Recorder's finding that the Box weighed between 7.5 and 8kg, contrary to the Defendant's pleaded case that it weighed 6.4kg. The Guidance suggests that when lifting a load, which is easy to grasp with both hands and weighs 7kg or more, off the floor to mid-calf height, a detailed risk assessment is necessary.

The Defendant submits that these grounds wrongly pre-suppose that the Claimant had satisfied the Recorder that there was a real

> ***risk of injury. In fact, he was not so satisfied and in those circumstances no detailed risk assessment was necessary.***
>
> *I agree with the Defendant that on a proper analysis of the Recorder's judgment he was finding that there was no real risk of injury. At [36] the Recorder found that:*
>
> > *"Given the nature, design and weight of the box or carry case involved here and the absence of any complaints, suggestion or evidence of any sort that it had posed any difficulties for midwives of any age, the vast majority of whom were women, over a number of years of regular use,* ***I am not convinced, on the balance of probabilities, that any risk assessment beyond the implicit formation of a view that it was safe if properly handled was required by the Defendant.*** *That is effectively what Mrs Moulla described as the position here."*

<u>*Assault at Work* –</u> RHY CLIVE BELLMAN v NORTHAMPTON RECRUITMENT LTD (2018)

An appeal from the order of His Honour Judge Cotter QC dated 13 December 2016. It raises the issue of the scope of vicarious liability in circumstances where an employee's wrongful conduct occurs outside the workplace and outside office hours. The Judge dismissed the Appellant's claim having decided that the Respondent company was not vicariously liable for the conduct of its managing director, Mr John Major. The case said:-

> *Having considered the relevant authorities to which his attention had been drawn, the Judge turned to apply the principles to the facts. He addressed Mr Major's field of activity at [65] – [67] of his judgment and came to the conclusions about Mr Major's role and authority to which I have referred at paragraph 2 above. The Judge concluded at [68] as follows:*

> ***"However it cannot be right that the effect of such a wide range and duration of duties is that Mr Major could always be considered to be on, or potentially on duty, solely because he was in the company of other employees regardless of circumstances."***

Grounds of Appeal

11. The grounds of appeal are that the Judge was wrong to hold that there was insufficient connection between the position in which Mr Major was employed and his wrongful conduct to make it right that NR should be liable under the principle of social justice. *Further,* ***in coming to that conclusion the Judge failed to take account of: the nature of Mr Major's job as managing director and the power and authority entrusted to him over subordinate employees; the fact that the wrongful conduct was triggered by a challenge to his managerial authority; whether the conduct was personal rather than connected to Mr Major's employment; that the risk of the wrongful conduct was enhanced by NR's provision of alcohol;*** *and* ***that he wrongly concluded that the imposition of vicarious liability for conduct in such circumstances would be potentially uninsurable and would place an undue burden on the employer.***

In summary, it seems to me that given the whole context, and despite the time and place at which the assault occurred, ***Mr Major's position of seniority persisted and was a significant factor. He was in a dominant position and had a supervisory role which enabled him to assert his authority over the staff who were present and to re- assert that authority when he thought it necessary.*** *Of course, his position was different from that of the police officer in Bernard v Attorney General of Jamaica [2004] UKPC 47 and the army officer in Ministry of Defence v Radclyffe [2009] EWCA Civ 635. In the former case, although it was not known whether the police officer was on duty when the shooting occurred it was common ground that he was allowed to exercise his powers outside his assigned hours of duty: see [14]. Nevertheless, it was considered to be of prime importance* *that the shooting incident followed immediately upon the officer's announcement that he was a policeman which was probably calculated to create the impression that he was on police business: see [25].* ***In all the circumstances, therefore, as a matter of law, having conducted an evaluative judgment based upon the primary facts as found, there is sufficient connection between Mr Major's field of activities and the assault to render it just that NR should be vicariously liable for his actions.***

COSH UPDATE – DOUGLAS FORD v (1) NORTHERN RAIL LTD (2) QBE INSURANCE (EUROPE) LTD (2018)

The claimant, who is the respondent to this appeal, sought damages for personal injury, alleging that he had developed occupational asthma as a result of exposure to paint fumes in the course of his employment. The case said-

The defendants are the claimant's former employer and their insurers. The defendants had admitted breach of duty but causation remained in issue. The value of the claim, if it succeeded, also remained to be determined. Therefore, the issues for the recorder at trial were causation and quantum, that is valuation.

Regrettably, I have come to the conclusion that the recorder failed to engage with the issue of causation. He appears to have approached it as being a foregone conclusion, when a proper analysis was that it was a live issue, dependent upon a finding that the claimant had been subject to meaningful exposure to isocyanates. The recorder's approach led him into error whereby his very clear conclusion at para.60 that the claimant had suffered occupational asthma as a result of exposure to isocyanate was unreasoned and unstained.

The claimant points to evidence from his expert engineer, who, as I have said, was not called to give oral evidence, that if heat was used the levels "could readily exceed the maximum exposure limit" and that "the exposures of the claimant could foreseeably have been in excess of the MEL(maximum exposure limit)". That evidence did provide the possibility that the claimant was exposed to a level of isocyanates that may have caused his asthma. However, it did not, in my judgment, establish that was probably the case.

34 I have considered whether, in the circumstances, I ought to remit the case for rehearing. Neither party urges me to do that, which is entirely understandable. In any event, I do not think it is necessary. ***Considering the evidence before the recorder, which I have in writing, including the transcript of the oral evidence, it is my judgment that the claimant was not able to prove his case on causation on a balance of probability. The most that could be established was that his asthma may have been caused by isocyanate exposure. That is not sufficient. Regrettably, therefore, I am bound to conclude that the claimant had not proved his case on causation. I must, therefore, overturn the recorder's decision and conclude that his claim should be dismissed.***

CHAPTER SEVEN
THE PI CLAIMS MARKET – AN OVERVIEW OF THE CHANGES

With the changes to the CMC market well under way, there will also be changes implemented to the Solicitor PI market. Jackson LJ said in July 2017:-

> *"Introduction*
>
> *In my January 2010 report, I recommended Fixed Recoverable Costs (FRC) for 'fast track' cases (claims up to £25,000 which can be tried in one day) and costs budgeting for 'multi-track' cases (bigger claims). I also said that we would need to look again at fixing costs for cases in the lower regions of the multi-track, once the reforms which I was then recommending had bedded in.*
>
> *Those reforms have now bedded in, although some fast track cases still do not have FRC. Therefore, it is now opportune to consider extending FRC. To that end, on 11th November 2016 the Lord Chief Justice and the Master of the Rolls commissioned me to carry out a further review, to develop proposals for extending FRC"*

https://www.judiciary.gov.uk/publications/review-of-civil-litigation-costs-supplemental-report-fixed-recoverable-costs/

This book is going to focus on the proposed changes to the Personal Injury Solicitor Marketplace between now and 2019 including:-

1. Fixed costs in almost all fast track cases and the 'intermediate' track. The report said:-

"I recommend a grid of FRC for all fast track cases, as set out in chapter 5. Above the fast track, I recommend a new 'intermediate' track for certain claims up to £100,000 which can be tried in three days or less, with no more than two expert witnesses giving oral evidence on each side. The intermediate track will have streamlined procedures and a grid of FRC".

The fixed costs tables and bands are set out as below:-

Band 1: RTA non-personal injury, defended debt cases.

Band 2: RTA personal injury (within Protocol), holiday sickness claims.

Band 3: RTA personal injury (outside Protocol), ELA, PL, tracked possession claims, housing disrepair, other money claims.

Band 4: ELD claims (other than NIHL), any particularly complex tracked possession claims or housing disrepair claims, property disputes, professional negligence claims and other claims at the top end of the fast track.

Matrix of FRC for fast track claims (applies to both claimant and defendant recoverable costs)

<table>
<tr><td></td><td colspan="4">Complexity Band</td></tr>
<tr><td>Stage:</td><td>1</td><td>2</td><td>3</td><td>4</td></tr>
<tr><td>Pre-issue £1,001-£5,000</td><td></td><td>£104 + 20% of damages</td><td>£988 + 17.5% of damages</td><td rowspan="3">£2,250 + 15% of damages + £440 per extra defendant</td></tr>
<tr><td>Pre-issue £5,001-£10,000</td><td></td><td>£1,144 + 15% of damages over £5,000</td><td>£1,929 + 12.5% of damages over £5,000</td></tr>
<tr><td>Pre-issue £10,001-£25,000</td><td>£500</td><td>£2,007 + 10% of damages over £10,000</td><td>£2,600 + 10% of damages over £10,000</td></tr>
<tr><td>Post-issue, pre-allocation</td><td>£1,850</td><td>£1,206 + 20% of damages</td><td>£2,735 + 20% of damages</td><td>£2,575 + 40% of damages + £660 per extra defendant</td></tr>
<tr><td>Post-allocation, pre-listing</td><td>£2,200</td><td>£1,955 + 20% of damages</td><td>£3,484 + 25% of damages</td><td>£5,525 + 40% of damages + £660 per extra defendant</td></tr>
<tr><td>Post-listing, pre- trial</td><td>£3,250</td><td>£2,761 + 20% of damages</td><td>£4,451 + 30% of damages</td><td>£6,800 + 40% of damages + £660 per extra defendant</td></tr>
<tr><td>Trial advocacy fee11</td><td>a. £500 b. £710 c. £1,070 d. £1,705</td><td>a. £500 b. £710 c. £1,070 d. £1,705</td><td>a. £500 b. £710 c. £1,070 d. £1,705</td><td>a. £1,380 b. £1,380 c. £1,800 d. £2,500</td></tr>
</table>

2. Clinical Negligence Fixed costs. The report said:-

"Clinical negligence claims are often of low financial value, but of huge concern to the individuals on both sides. The complexity of such cases means that they are usually unsuited to either the fast track or my proposed intermediate track. ***In chapter 8, I recommend that the Department of Health and the Civil Justice Council should set up a working party with both claimant and defendant representatives to develop a bespoke***

process for handling clinical negligence claims up to £25,000. That bespoke process should have a grid of FRC attached. *This scheme will capture most clinical negligence claims. Previous experience (for example, with noise induced hearing loss claims) shows that it is possible for the 'industry' to come together and develop such schemes. There is sufficient good will on both sides to achieve that in the field of clinical negligence. I remain willing to arbitrate informally on any points of disagreement.*

3. Increases to the Small Claims Track and a Ban on Pre Medical Offers. The report sets out:-

   "3.10 Whiplash reforms. On 23rd February 2017, the Government published part one of its responses to the consultation, "Reforming the soft tissue injury ('whiplash') claims process", which closed on 6th January 2017.15 ***This included a number of reforms, including the introduction of a tariff of fixed compensation for pain, suffering and loss of amenity for injuries with a duration of less than two years. Further reforms include a ban on settlement of claims without medical evidence, increasing the small claims limit for RTA related personal injury claims to £5,000, and increasing the small claims limit for all other types of personal injury claims to £2,000. The current limit for these types of claim is £1,000. The aim of these reforms is to disincentivise minor, exaggerated and fraudulent road traffic accident related soft-tissue claims, leading to projected overall savings to insurers of £1bn.*** *The Government included clauses on these reforms in the Prison and Court Reform Bill, before the June General Election necessitated the dissolution of Parliament. In the Queen's Speech on 21st June, the new Government stated its intention to proceed with whiplash reform by a new Civil Liability Bill?"*

4. A Tariff System for RTA Claims. The MOJ report on the PI Whiplash consultation proposes the following for RTA claims at:-

https://www.gov.uk/government/uploads/system/uploads/attachment_data/file/593431/part-1-response-to-reforming-soft-tissue-injury-claims.pdf

The Government has decided that the levels of compensation available under the new tariff will be as follows:

Injury Duration	2015 average payment for PSLA – uplifted to take account of JCG uplift (industry data)	JC guidelines	New tariff amounts
0–3 months	£1,750	A few hundred pounds to £2,050	£225
4–6 months	£2,150	£2,050 to £3,630	£450
7–9 months	£2,600	£2,050 to £3,630	£765
10–12 months	£3,100	£2,050 to £3,630	£1,190
13–15 months	£3,500	£3,630 to £6,600	£1,820
16–18 months	£3,950	£3,630 to £6,600	£2,660
19–24 months	£4,500	£3,630 to £6,600	£3,725

5. Online Courts, the Jackson Supplemental report said:-

> ***Online Solutions Court. The Online Solutions Court will be a new court, separate from the County Court, intended for litigants to use without recourse to legal representation. It will have a simplified procedure and a strictly limited FRC regime.*** *It will deal with matters up to a value of £25,000 (including cases that currently fall within both the small claims track and the fast track).* ***However, fast track personal injury, clinical negligence, possession, intellectual property and housing disrepair claims will be excluded from its remit, as will any other case which is too complex for proper resolution within the Online Solutions Court. Such cases (with the exception of intellectual property cases) will remain in the Fast Track in the County Court.*** *Those remaining cases will be subject to the rules proposed in Chapter 5 above. In this way, the Online Solutions Court and the fast track will sit side by side, subjecting all claims below £25,000 to some form of fixed costs recovery.*

The Jackson report sets out:-

> ***1.2 The holy grail. The holy grail pursued by every civil justice reformer is a system in which the actual costs of each party are a modest fraction of the sum in issue, and the winner recovers those modest costs from the loser.*** *Germany comes closer to the ideal than we do, because it has a civil justice system fundamentally different from our own, with little disclosure and little oral evidence.1* ***In the context of a common law jurisdiction, however, there are limits on what can be achieved. Adversarial litigation is an inherently expensive process.***
>
> *1.3 What is achievable in the real world? The best that can be achieved is:*
>
> > *(i) to modify the procedural rules with the aim of reducing the actual costs so far as possible;*

(ii) to restrict recoverable costs to that which is 'proportionate' as defined in the new proportionality rule;2 and

(iii) to control the recoverable costs in advance

What does this all mean the in real world for PI Lawyers?

1. Costs will be fixed in most cases and more cases will be pushed into the small claims track.

2. Fixed costs will be extended into the multi track/ new intermediate track.

3. RTA claims are now sought to be restricted without the help from a Lawyer.

4. We will likely see an expansion of the online Courts.

5. The Jackson report will seek to simply some of the rules (as set out in later Chapters).

These are uncertain times for personal injury lawyers. It is clear that for the moment EL/PL/ housing and more complex PI claims will still be costs bearing. PI Lawyers must diversify in this new market place beyond RTA claims. An RTA claims market will only work for large volumes of claims but EL/PL/ housing disrepair and more complex PI claims will remain profitable for the foreseeable future. How long before further changes will be placed upon the PI market beyond these changes remains to be seen. For the time being, PI and Clinical Negligence lawyers have plenty to be getting on with.

MORE BOOKS BY LAW BRIEF PUBLISHING

A selection of our other titles available now:-

'A Practical Guide to Prison Injury Claims' by Malcolm Johnson
'A Practical Guide to Hackney Carriage Licensing in London' by Stuart Jessop
'A Practical Guide to Advising Clients at the Police Station' by Colin Stephen McKeown-Beaumont
'A Practical Guide to Antisocial Behaviour Injunctions' by by Iain Wightwick
'A Practical Guide to TOLATA Claims' by Greg Williams
'Planning Obligations Demystified: A Practical Guide to Planning Obligations and Section 106 Agreements' by Bob Mc Geady & Meyric Lewis
'A Practical Guide to Agricultural Law and Tenancies' by Christopher McNall
'A Practical Guide to Crofting Law' by Brian Inkster
'A Practical Guide to Spousal Maintenance' by Liz Cowell
'A Practical Guide to the Law of Domain Names and Cybersquatting' by Andrew Clemson
'A Practical Guide to the Law of Gender Pay Gap Reporting' by Harini Iyengar
'Ellis and Kevan on Credit Hire – 5th Edition' by Aidan Ellis & Tim Kevan
'Artificial Intelligence – The Practical Legal Issues' by John Buyers
'A Practical Guide to the Rights of Grandparents in Children Proceedings' by Stuart Barlow
'NHS Whistleblowing and the Law' by Joseph England
'Employment Law and the Gig Economy' by Nigel Mackay & Annie Powell
'A Practical Guide to the General Data Protection Regulation (GDPR)' by Keith Markham
'A Practical Guide to Noise Induced Hearing Loss (NIHL) Claims' by Andrew Mckie, Ian Skeate, Gareth McAloon

'An Introduction to Beauty Negligence Claims – A Practical Guide for the Personal Injury Practitioner' by Greg Almond
'Intercompany Agreements for Transfer Pricing Compliance' by Paul Sutton
'Zen and the Art of Mediation' by Martin Plowman
'A Practical Guide to the SRA Principles, Individual and Law Firm Codes of Conduct 2019 – What Every Law Firm Needs to Know' by Paul Bennett
'A Practical Guide to Licensing Law for Commercial Property Lawyers' by Niall McCann & Richard Williams
'A Practical Guide to Adoption for Family Lawyers' by Graham Pegg
'Essential Motor Finance Law for the Busy Practitioner' by Richard Humphreys
'A Practical Guide to Industrial Disease Claims' by Andrew Mckie & Ian Skeate
'A Practical Guide to the Law of Armed Conflict' by Jo Morris & Libby Anderson
'A Practical Guide to Redundancy' by Philip Hyland
'A Practical Guide to Vicarious Liability' by Mariel Irvine
'A Practical Guide to Claims Arising from Delays in Diagnosing Cancer' by Bella Webb
'A Practical Guide to Applications for Landlord's Consent and Variation of Leases' by Mark Shelton
'A Practical Guide to Relief from Sanctions Post-Mitchell and Denton' by Peter Causton
'Butler's Equine Tax Planning: 2nd Edition' by Julie Butler
'A Practical Guide to Equity Release for Advisors' by Paul Sams
'A Practical Guide to Unlawful Eviction and Harassment' by Stephanie Lovegrove
'A Practical Guide to the Law Relating to Food' by Ian Thomas
'A Practical Guide to the Ending of Assured Shorthold Tenancies' by Elizabeth Dwomoh
'A Practical Guide to Financial Services Claims' by Chris Hegarty
'The Law of Houses in Multiple Occupation: A Practical Guide to HMO Proceedings' by Julian Hunt
'A Practical Guide to Unlawful Eviction and Harassment' by Stephanie Lovegrove
'A Practical Guide to Solicitor and Client Costs' by Robin Dunne

'A Practical Guide to Wrongful Conception, Wrongful Birth and Wrongful Life Claims' by Rebecca Greenstreet
'Occupiers, Highways and Defective Premises Claims: A Practical Guide Post-Jackson – 2nd Edition' by Andrew Mckie
'A Practical Guide to Financial Ombudsman Service Claims' by Adam Temple & Robert Scrivenor
'A Practical Guide to the Law of Enfranchisement and Lease Extension' by Paul Sams
'A Practical Guide to Marketing for Lawyers – 2nd Edition' by Catherine Bailey & Jennet Ingram
'A Practical Guide to Advising Schools on Employment Law' by Jonathan Holden
'Certificates of Lawful Use and Development: A Guide to Making and Determining Applications' by Bob Mc Geady & Meyric Lewis
'A Practical Guide to the Law of Dilapidations' by Mark Shelton
'A Guide to Consent in Clinical Negligence Post-Montgomery' by Lauren Sutherland QC
'A Practical Guide to Running Housing Disrepair and Cavity Wall Claims: 2nd Edition' by Andrew Mckie & Ian Skeate
'A Practical Guide to Digital and Social Media Law for Lawyers' by Sherree Westell
'A Practical Guide to Holiday Sickness Claims – 2nd Edition' by Andrew Mckie & Ian Skeate
'A Practical Guide to Elderly Law' by Justin Patten
'Arguments and Tactics for Personal Injury and Clinical Negligence Claims' by Dorian Williams
'A Practical Guide to QOCS and Fundamental Dishonesty' by James Bentley
'A Practical Guide to Drone Law' by Rufus Ballaster, Andrew Firman, Eleanor Clot
'Practical Mediation: A Guide for Mediators, Advocates, Advisers, Lawyers, and Students in Civil, Commercial, Business, Property, Workplace, and Employment Cases' by Jonathan Dingle with John Sephton
'A Practical Guide to Compliance for Personal Injury Firms Working With Claims Management Companies' by Paul Bennett
'A Practical Guide to the Landlord and Tenant Act 1954: Commercial Tenancies' by Richard Hayes & David Sawtell
'A Practical Guide to Psychiatric Claims in Personal Injury' by Liam Ryan

'A Practical Guide to Dog Law for Owners and Others' by Andrea Pitt
'RTA Allegations of Fraud in a Post-Jackson Era: The Handbook – 2nd Edition' by Andrew Mckie
'RTA Personal Injury Claims: A Practical Guide Post-Jackson' by Andrew Mckie
'On Experts: CPR35 for Lawyers and Experts' by David Boyle
'An Introduction to Personal Injury Law' by David Boyle
'A Practical Guide to Claims Arising From Accidents Abroad and Travel Claims' by Andrew Mckie & Ian Skeate
'A Practical Guide to Chronic Pain Claims' by Pankaj Madan
'A Practical Guide to Claims Arising from Fatal Accidents' by James Patience
'A Practical Approach to Clinical Negligence Post-Jackson' by Geoffrey Simpson-Scott
'Employers' Liability Claims: A Practical Guide Post-Jackson' by Andrew Mckie
'A Practical Guide to Subtle Brain Injury Claims' by Pankaj Madan
'The Law of Driverless Cars: An Introduction' by Alex Glassbrook
'A Practical Guide to Costs in Personal Injury Cases' by Matthew Hoe
'The No Nonsense Solicitors' Practice: A Guide To Running Your Firm' by Bettina Brueggemann
'The Queen's Counsel Lawyer's Omnibus: 20 Years of Cartoons from The Times 1993-2013' by Alex Steuart Williams

These books and more are available to order online direct from the publisher at www.lawbriefpublishing.com, where you can also read free sample chapters. For any queries, contact us on 0844 587 2383 or mail@lawbriefpublishing.com.

Our books are also usually in stock at www.amazon.co.uk with free next day delivery for Prime members, and at good legal bookshops such as Wildy & Sons.

We are regularly launching new books in our series of practical day-to-day practitioners' guides. Visit our website and join our free newsletter to be kept informed and to receive special offers, free chapters, etc.

You can also follow us on Twitter at www.twitter.com/lawbriefpub.

www.ingramcontent.com/pod-product-compliance
Lightning Source LLC
LaVergne TN
LVHW022102200926
848481LV00003B/1030